# DUMPED!

## FUN AND GAMES

# ACTIVITY BOOK

Featuring
word Scrambles,
Connect-the-Dots, and
In-Depth Psychiatric
Analysis for the
Unexpectedly Single

Josh Lewis



adamsmedia
avon, massachusetts

Published by
Adams Media, an F+W Media Company
57 Littlefield Street, Avon, MA 02322. U.S.A.
www.adamsmedia.com

ISBN 10: 1-59869-562-2
ISBN 13: 978-1-59869-562-5

Printed in the United States of America.

J I H G F E D C B A

Library of Congress Cataloging-in-Publication Data is available from the publisher.



This book is available at quantity discounts for bulk purchases. For information, please call 1-800-289-0963.

# Samantha's Story

This is Samantha.

Samantha just got dumped.

Come on out. It's okay.
Sometimes sunshine is nice.
Grrrrr.
Looks like we have our work cut out for us.

Will you help coax Samantha out of her dark and scary cave of despair and stand by her as she journeys towards the exhilarating and empowering highway of sanity?

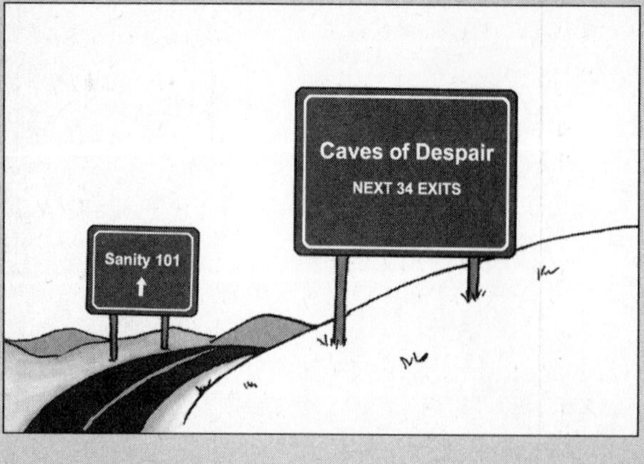
Caves of Despair
NEXT 34 EXITS
Sanity 101

Time's a wastin'! Let's begin.

# Mixed Emotions

He could be so great sometimes, but sometimes he was Satan. God, I miss him.
I'm sorry—I was focused on your roots—did you just say you miss Satan?

For Samantha, being involved with her ex has always involved a wide variety of emotions. Even though they're not together anymore, Samantha's emotions are still just as jumbled up as ever.

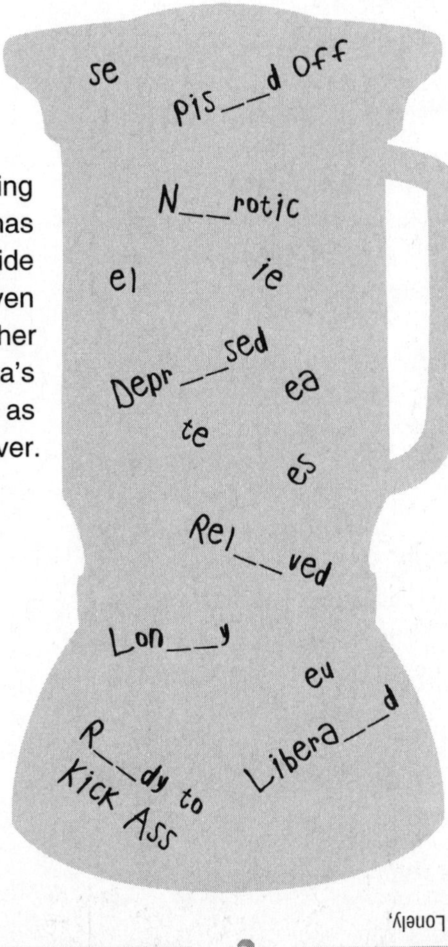
se
pis__d Off
N__rotic
el
ie
Depr__sed
ea
te
es
Rel__ved
Lon__y
eu
R__dy to Kick Ass
Libera__d

Help Samantha sort out her emotions while she makes herself an extra-thick chocolate shake. Take the letters from the blender and place them in front of the appropriate words.

Answers: Neurotic, Depressed, Relieved, Lonely, Pissed Off, Liberated, Ready to Kick Ass

# International Relations

An important thing for Samantha to understand is that she's not alone. People all over the world go through breakups every day. Below are ten people from all around the world who've been dumped. Help Samantha match up the dumped people with their countries of origin from the globe below.

-------------- 1. My ex broke up with me while we were eating raw fish and drinking rice wine. Despite my country's strong work ethic and mastery of high technology, nothing could prepare me for the sting of heartbreak.

-------------- 2. My country used to be one of the two great superpowers in the world. When communism fell, so did my relationship.

-------------- 3. I like to eat rich foods, wear hats on the side of my head, and smoke a lot. My country invented kissing with the tongue. Unfortunately, I don't do that anymore . . . not since mon amour gave me zee boot!

-------------- 4. In my country, we speak while gesturing violently with our hands. And we love pasta! When my ex broke up with me, we screamed a lot. But we scream a lot in my country even when we're not breaking up. Ciao!

-------------- 5. My country is one of the oldest civilizations in the world. We have pyramids and the world's longest river and a woman named Dendera who will no longer take my phone calls.

-------------- 6. We have more than 1 billion people in my country, and I've been dumped by at least half of them.

-------------- 7. Where I come from, some of us speak English and some of us speak French. My ex dumped me in both.

-------------- 8. All I ever do since my ex broke up with me is take a lot of drugs and sleep with hookers. Luckily, all of that is legal where I live!

-------------- 9. In my country, we like spicy foods and even spicier love. But if you come to my country, stay away from the water, and stay away from Juan! They'll both lure you in and then leave you with dysentery.

-------------- 10. G'day, mate! I hope you like kangaroos and koalas, because we've got a lot of them in my country. We've also got a lot of barbies . . . although my tosser, nob-sucker of an ex took mine.

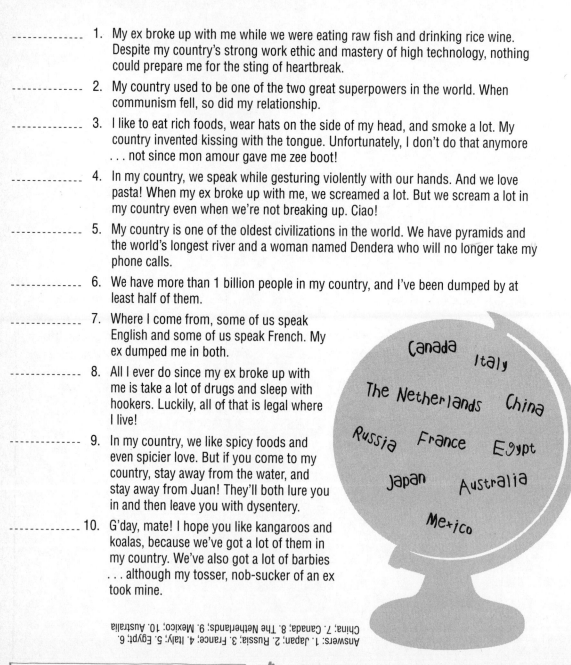

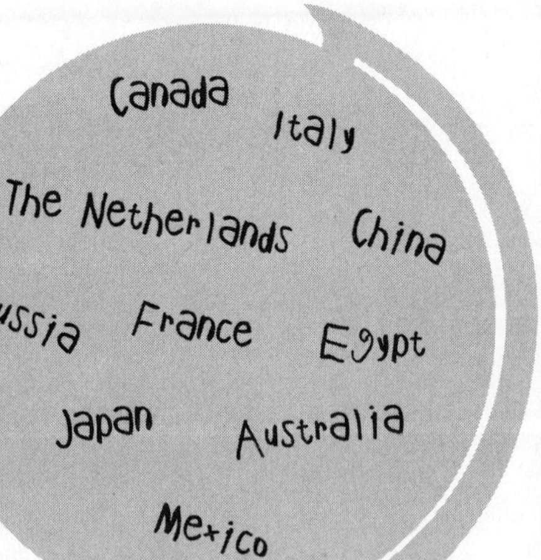
Canada
Italy
The Netherlands
China
Russia
France
Egypt
Japan
Australia
Mexico

Answers: 1. Japan; 2. Russia; 3. France; 4. Italy; 5. Egypt; 6. China; 7. Canada; 8. The Netherlands; 9. Mexico; 10. Australia

# Breakup Breakdown

Help Samantha cut through her ex's breakup jibber-jabber!

Breakups can be very confusing affairs, to say the least. Dumpers often disguise their real reasons for dropping the breakup bomb. Use the Dumped Decoder to help Samantha discover a major element in her ex's reasons for letting her go. Fill in the appropriate blank words below that her ex used to "let her down easy." Once you've done that, place the letters from the parentheses in order on the line at the bottom of the page to help Samantha find a hidden message in his words.

1. ( ___ ) ___ ' ___ not you, it's me.
2. I know I'm making the greatest ( ___ ) ___ ___ ___ ___ ___ ___ of my life.
3. You will always have a place in my ___ ___ ( ___ ) ___ ___.
4. You're ___ ___ ___ ___ ( ___ ) to find some great guy and be married in no time, you'll see.
5. I ___ ( ___ ) ___ ___ I could be worthy of you.
6. We had some ___ ___ ___ ( ___ ) ___ times.
7. There's nothing I ___ ___ ___ ___ ___ ( ___ ) ' ___ do for you.
8. We gave ___ ( ___ ) one heck of a try.
9. This is going to hurt me ( ___ ) ___ ___ ___ ___ than it's going to hurt you.
10. I need to find my place in the ___ ___ ( ___ ) ___ ___ ___ ___ ___.
11. Don't think of this as the end, think of it as a ___ ( ___ ) ___ beginning.
12. I need you so bad, and that's my problem: I have to ___ ___ ___ ___ ( ___ ) how to not need you.
13. Please don't ever ___ ___ ___ ___ ( ___ ) ___ me.
14. Would it be ___ ( ___ ) ___ ___ ___ for us to do it one last time?

**SECRET MESSAGE:**

___ ' ___ ___ ___ ___ ___ ___ ___ ___ ___ ___ ___ ___ ___ ___ ___ ___

Words: It's, mistake, heart, going, wish, great, wouldn't, it, worse, universe, new, learn, forget, wrong

Answer: I'm a giant wiener.

# State of the Disunion Address

Now that Samantha's had some time to let the reality of her breakup sink in, it's time for her to notify the people.

Samantha has a statement all prepared, but some of the words have gotten mixed up. In all, there are twenty-four words in the wrong place. Each out-of-place word has accidentally been switched with another out-of-place word within the statement. Help Samantha sort out her thoughts by writing the proper words on the lines next to the out-of-place words and crossing out the incorrect words.

Answers: After seven-and-a-half years of (devotion) to each other, my boyfriend and I have (elected) to finally call it (quits). While I will (reflect) upon these past seven-and-a-half years with (fondness), the fact is that they were often (fraught) with controversy. I realize this news might come as a (blow) to some of you, but I (guarantee) you that it's the right (decision) for us at this point in time. I'm not (bitter). Really, I'm not. In fact, I feel (amazing). I haven't felt this good in (hmm) . . . let me see . . . seven-and-a-half years! It feels (exhilarating) to be free after all this time. So you don't need to be (concerned) about me, because I'm (good). In fact, I might go out and get (laid) right now. That's right! You (heard) me! Maybe I'll go out and (mount) the first guy I see, just because I can. I don't even give a (crap) who he is. He could be a six-headed (felon) from (Krypton) for all I care. It doesn't matter, 'cuz I got my (mojo) working and I need to get me some! In fact, that's (exactly) what I'm going to go do now! By the way, if you run into my ex, please tell him that he's a (motherfucker)!

**STATEMENT**

After seven-and-a-half years of **good** _________ to each other, my boyfriend and I have **amazing** _________ to finally call it **crap** _________. While I will **blow** _________ upon these past seven-and-a-half years with **mojo** _________, the fact is that they were often **mount** _________ with controversy. I realize this news might come as a **reflect** _________ to some of you, but I **laid** _________ you that it's the right **exactly** _________ for us at this point in time. I'm not **Krypton** _________. Really, I'm not. In fact, I feel **elected** _________. I haven't felt this good in **felon** _________ . . . let me see . . . seven-and-a-half years! It feels **motherfucker** _________ to be free after all this time. So you don't need to be **heard** _________ about me, because I'm **devotion** _________. In fact, I might go out and get **guarantee** _________ right now. That's right! You **concerned** _________ me! Maybe I'll go out and **fraught** _________ the first guy I see, just because I can. I don't give a **quits** _________ who he is. He could be a six-headed **hmm** _________ from **bitter** _________ for all I care. It doesn't matter, 'cuz I got my **fondness** _________ working and I need to get me some! In fact, that's **decision** _________ what I'm going to go do now! By the way, if you run into my ex, please tell him that he's a **exhilarating** _________!

# Checkered Past

It's reflection time! As much as she'd like to believe that everything between her and her ex was peachy keen until very recently, the truth is, their troubles go way back.

Does this water make me look fat?
Yes.

Help Samantha look back at key moments from their relationship and attach a year to the events in order to help get some perspective. On the facing page are nine scenarios that happened between Samantha and her ex. There's one for each year they were together starting in the year **2000** and ending in **2008**. Write the appropriate year in the box for each scenario.

| | | |
|---|---|---|
| Scenario 1 | Scenario 2 | Scenario 3 |
| Scenario 4 | Scenario 5 | Scenario 6 |
| Scenario 7 | Scenario 8 | Scenario 9 |

## Scenarios

1. **Samantha:** Why can't we watch what I want to watch for once?

   **Ex:** We can. I just don't want to watch that idiotic new Idol show. It's going to get canceled in like a week.

2. **Samantha:** I'm not saying I need to get married tomorrow. I'm just saying we should at least discuss the possibility.

   **Ex:** I want to discuss it! But why you gotta be bustin' my chops about it now, while Saddam Hussein is building up his arsenal of weapons of mass destruction? Are you an American or what? Jeez!

3. **Samantha:** So now, all of a sudden, you never want to have a family?

   **Ex:** I didn't say *never*! But why you gotta be bustin' my chops about it now, when the U.S. report on Iraq found NO weapons of mass destruction. Aren't you worried about our government and its relationship with the truth? Jeez!

4. **Samantha:** It's at times like this that I feel so lucky to have you. What are Tom and Nicole going to do now without each other?

5. **Samantha:** You always do this. Whenever it's something that you want me to do with you, I'm there. But when it's one of my friends, you always suddenly have plans.

   **Ex:** That's not true. I was really looking forward to Suzie and Ed's baby shower. But Rick's super broken up about the whole Britney Spears shaved head thing, and he really needs me now. Besides, it's not like Suzie won't get pregnant again.

6. **Samantha:** It's at times like this that I feel so lucky to have you. What are Brad and Jen going to do now without each other?

   **Ex:** He's with Angelina Jolie now.

   **Samantha:** Oh . . . that was fast.

   **Ex:** If you ask me, he upgraded. Did you see *Tomb Raider* . . . Grrrowlll!

7. **Samantha:** When are you finally going to grow up?

   **Ex:** Okay, I'm not perfect! But at least I'm not Mel Gibson. I'd never get drunk and tell you "the Jews are responsible for all the wars in the world."

8. **Samantha:** We're going to a Hannah Montana concert for my birthday?

   **Ex:** Hey, she's not just for kids. Did you see those *Vanity Fair* photos? Yowza!

9. **Samantha:** I must be dreaming. I can't believe I met you and Al Gore was elected president, all in the same night.

Answers: 1. 2002; 2. 2003; 3. 2004; 4. 2001; 5. 2007; 6. 2005; 7. 2006; 8. 2008; 9. 2000

# Going Up?: Volume 1

Samantha's not feeling so hot. Looks like it might be a good time for Samantha to take a ride in the uplift elevators!

Samantha is going to take a ride in the "Un Elevator." The catch is the Un Elevator only has one floor that Samantha should visit. All of the other floors would only make Samantha feel worse. Take a close look at all of the buttons in the Un Elevator and color in the one that you think would be best for Samantha.

## Un-

| | | | | |
|---|---|---|---|---|
| happy | reachable | desirable | conscious | derachieving |
| even | certain | clogged | comfortable | derfed |
| able | american | aware | decided | hinged |
| armed | animous | bearable | defeated | kempt |
| affected | appealing | circumcised | cool | ruly |

Answer: Undefeated

# Some Kind of Dink!: The Ol' Switcheroo

One of Samantha's ex's greatest skills was his ability to take Samantha's words and twist them around to suit his needs. Now that Samantha has some distance, help her to revisit some of these instances so that she can recognize this pattern and avoid it in the future.

Below are examples of how Samantha's ex, with very little effort, took the letters from her words, mixed them up, and spit them back out to suit his needs. Fill in the blanks for the words Samantha said and then fill in the words that her ex turned her words into.

EVLO
Check it out! I turned "love" into "evlo."
That's great.
You need to get a hobby, man.

1. **Samantha:** How could you ________ me like that in front of your friends?
   **Ex:** You know, you've got the cutest little ________.
2. **Samantha:** This is the ________ time I wait to eat dinner with you. You said you'd be home three hours ago.
   **Ex:** Would you pass the ________?
3. **Samantha:** It's bad enough that you were flirting with another girl in front of me, but a sixteen year old? How can you ________ with yourself?
   **Ex:** First of all, she was seventeen. Second of all, I wasn't flirting. And third of all, even if I was, what's the big deal? You're acting like I'm ________ incarnate.
4. **Samantha:** I'm going to ________ out with my parents for brunch, and they made a point of inviting you along.
   **Ex:** Oh yea, thanks, sounds great, but I think I'll pass. I wouldn't want to be a ________.
5. **Samantha:** I hate it when you ________ me on the ass in front of people.
   **Ex:** Relax . . . I thought we were ________.
6. **Samantha:** We ________ to have a talk about the apartment and what we can do to make it more livable.
   **Ex:** What's there to talk about? We live in the Garden of friggin' ________.
7. **Samantha:** Would you please get out of that ________ already and get dressed? We're supposed to be at Bonnie's by seven.
   **Ex:** Your friends ________ me.
8. **Samantha:** I'm really getting sick of you treating me like ________ today.
   **Ex:** That's why I'm going fishing for ________ with Rex.
9. **Samantha:** I don't understand what the problem is. You know I have nothing but pure unadulterated ________ for you.
   **Ex:** Yea, I guess. Still, sometimes I just wish you were more of a ________.
10. **Samantha:** There's nothing you can do to ________ me anymore.
    **Ex:** Will you shave my ________ for me?

Answers: 1. snub/buns; 2. last/salt; 3. live/evil; 4. step/pest; 5. slap/pals; 6. need/Eden; 7. robe/bore; 8. crap/carp; 9. lust/slut; 10. stun/nuts

# Attract Fun

They say that opposites attract. Sure, they do. But opposites also get together and drive each other crazy before finally breaking up after years and years of turmoil that could've been prevented if they'd just realized to begin with that while opposites sometimes attract, that doesn't necessarily mean they stand a snowball's chance in hell of ever making it work.

One thing Samantha's friends believe has kept Samantha from landing in a stable long-term relationship (she's done the "long-term" part, but has yet to experience the "stable") is her inability to recognize compatibility when she sees it.

I just don't get what they see in each other.

Help Samantha improve her matchmaking skills so that she might eventually use them to find herself a suitable mate. To the right are quotes from twenty different people. Assist each person to find the right mate for them by drawing lines between them and the people they should be with.

1. **Woman:** I enjoy leather, bondage, and putting pathetic men in their places.
2. **Man:** The question of highway congestion will be obsolete by the year 2012 with the proliferation of PAMs—personal aviation modules.
3. **Man:** Nothing beats a tall glass of lemonade after mowing the lawn and building a birdhouse. Now that's what I call a perfect Sunday.
4. **Woman:** I just got through with a seventeen-hour hunger strike to protest the corruption of the bottled-water industry.
5. **Man:** I can't decide which I prefer, my dazzling smile or my perfect hair.
6. **Woman:** He, he, he. I like stuff. He, he, he.
7. **Woman:** There's this myth that women don't like having sex as much as guys. Fuck that! I haven't gotten laid in almost four hours and I'm climbing the friggin' walls.
8. **Man:** FINALLY! It's about time! American Apparel is opening a store down the street from me. HALLELUJAH! There is a God.
9. **Woman:** I call my latest installation, "Vaginal Detonation: A Meditation on Verisimilitude."
10. **Woman:** What the fuck are you looking at?

A. **Woman:** Gosh, I think these might be the tastiest snickerdoodles I've ever baked. Alrighty then, on to my sewing.

B. **Man:** My real name is Harold Walker, but my work name is Rock Dowel.

C. **Man:** I've worked hard for nearly fifty years. I've earned the right to marry whomever I want to. Even if she is fifteen years younger than my daughter.

D. **Man:** Cross me and I'll cut you.

E. **Woman:** My ass looks awesome in these jeans. That's just one of the many reasons why you want me.

F. **Woman:** Of course I love *Star Trek*, who doesn't? But I really feel *Quantum Leap* is an underrated classic.

G. **Woman:** The last guy that called my bike a Vespa is still in physical therapy.

H. **Man:** I've been a bad boy.

I. **Man:** There's no denying that Patti Lupone is one of the greatest performers ever to have graced a Broadway stage, but that doesn't change the fact that Bernadette Peters is without a doubt the First Lady of the American Musical Theater.

J. **Man:** I just wrote a new song. I call it "Goddamn I'm So Pissed Off at the World Because It Sucks."

Answers: 1. H; 2. F; 3. A; 4. J; 5. E; 6. C; 7. B; 8. I; 9. G; 10. D

# I Never Promised You a Rose Garden … Yes, You Did!

Samantha's ex promised Samantha that he'd be by her apartment at 3:00 to pick up his stuff. Samantha made a point of being at the apartment because her ex, in a very symbolic and overblown gesture, gave her his set of keys when he broke up with her and moved out.

It's 7:30, and Samantha's ex has yet to come by or call or make any contact whatsoever.

This is nothing new. From the very start of their relationship, Samantha's ex has been making promises to Samantha that he hasn't kept.

**Count the broken promises!**

On the facing page are all the broken promises Samantha's ex ever made to Samantha. Can you count them all up for Samantha so she can see once and for all what she's been putting up with all these years?

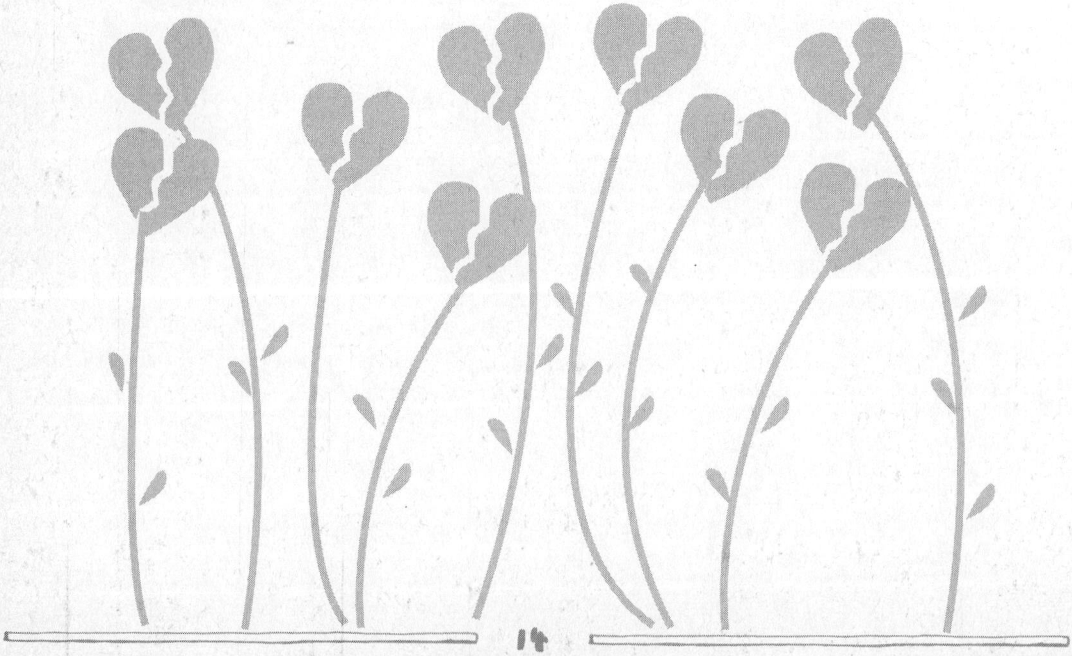

PRO MISE P RO MISE PR O MISE P RO MI SE PR OM ISE PR OM ISE PR OM I SE
P RO MI SE PR OM I S E PR OM IS E PROMISE P R O MI S E PROM IS E
PR O M ISE PRO MIS E PRO M ISE PRO M ISE PRO MISE PR OM ISE PRO M I S E
P ROM I SE PR O M IS E P ROM ISE PRO MI SE P ROMIS E PR O MIS E PROM IS E
PR O M I S E PROMISE PR O M I S E P R O M IS E P RO M I S E PRO MISE
P RO MISE PR O M ISE P RO MI SE PR OM ISE PR OM ISE PR OM I SE P RO MI SE
PR OM I S E PR OM IS E PRO MISE P R O MI S E PROM IS E PR O M ISE PRO MIS E
PRO PRO M ISE PRO MISE PR OM ISE PRO M I S E P ROM I SE PR O M IS E
P ROM ISE PRO MI SE PR O MIS E PROM IS E PR O M I S E PR OMISE PR O M I S E
P R O M IS E P RO M I S E PRO MISE P R O MI S E PROM IS E PR O M ISE
PRO MIS E PRO M ISE PRO M ISE PRO MISE PR OM ISE PRO M I S E P ROM I SE
PR O M IS E P ROM ISE PRO MI SE P RO MIS E PR O MIS E PROM IS E PR O M I S E
PRO M ISE PR O M I S E P R O M I S E P RO M I S E PRO MISEP RO MISE
PR O M ISE P RO MI SEPR OM ISE PR OM ISE PR OM I SE P RO MI SE PR OM I S E
P R OM IS EPRO MI E PRO MISE PR OM ISE PRO M I S E P ROM I S E PR O M IS E
SURROUNDED BYP ROM ISE PR O M I S E PR O M IS E P ROM ISE PRO MI SE
PR O MIS E PROM IS E PR O M I S E BROKEN PROMISE PR O M I S E P R O M IS E
P RO MISE P RO M I S E PRO PR O M ISE P RO MI SE PR OM ISE PR OM ISE
PR OM I SE P RO MI SE PR OM I S E PR OM IS E PROM ISE P R O MI S E PROM IS E
PR O M ISE PRO MIS E PRO MISE P R O MI SE PRO MISE P RO MISE PR O MISE
P RO MI SE PR OM ISE PR OM ISE PR OM I SE P RO MI SE PR OM I S E PR OM IS E
PROMISE P R O MI S E PROM IS E PR O M ISE PRO MIS E PRO M ISE PRO M ISE
PRO MISE PR OM ISE PRO M I S E P ROM I SE PR O M IS E P ROM ISE PRO MI SE
P ROMIS E PR O MIS E PROM IS E PR O M I S E PROMISE PR O M I S E
P R O M IS E P RO M I S E PRO MISE P RO MISE PR O M ISE P RO MI SE PR OM ISE
PR OM ISE PR OM I SE P RO MI SE PR OM I S E PR OM IS E PRO MISE P R O MI S E
PROM IS E PR O M ISE PRO MIS E PRO PRO M ISE PRO MISE PR OM ISE
PRO M I S E P ROM I SE PR O M IS E P ROM ISE PRO MI SE PR O MIS E PROM IS E
PR O M I S E PR OMISE PROM I S E P R O M IS E P RO M I S E PRO MISE
P R O MI S E PROM IS E PR O M ISE PRO MIS E PRO M ISE PRO M ISE
PRO MISE PR OM ISE PRO M I S E P ROM I SE PR O M IS E P ROM ISE
PRO MI SE P RO MIS E PR O MIS E PROM IS E PR O M I S E PRO M ISE

Answer: A lot.

# Breakout

One of the things Samantha's been struggling with recently is the whole idea of a "BREAK UP." A break implies something's broken.

When something's broken, you're supposed to fix it.

In this case, however, there's nothing to fix. The break has happened and it just has to stay broken. The thing that Samantha needs to do now is to take the "break," and use it to her advantage. Remember, "break" is a powerful word that can be used as the beginning or ending of all sorts of terrific words and phrases.

Help Samantha discover the many wonderful uses of break by figuring out the meanings of the pictures below. Each word or phrase includes the word "b-r-e-a-k" at either its beginning or ending.

1.  Break ___________

2.  Break ___________

3.  Break ___________

4.  ___________ Break

5. 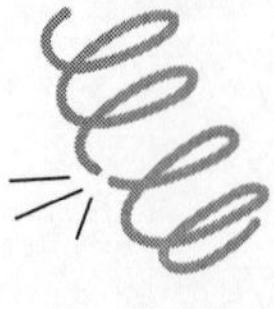 ___________ Break

Answers: 1. Break of day; 2. Break dance; 3. Break neck; 4. Coffee break; 5. Spring break

# Ass wackbards!

Samantha's having a tough day; she misses her ex, she feels lonely, and her self-esteem is running on empty.

Samantha wants to call her ex.

Samantha is starting to go backward. As a result, everything's getting flipped around. Get her to turn things around by reading the backward writing on the wall and helping her see things the right way. Turn the words on the wall around and write them in the blanks.

1. TNOD LLAC MIH ________ ________
2. ERUOY OOT DOOG ROF MIH ________ ________ ________ ________ ________
3. UOY KCOR ________ ________
4. EH SKCUS ________ ________

TNOD LLAC MIH
EH SKCUS
ERUOY OOT DOOG ROF MIH
UOY KCOR

Answers: 1. Don't call him. 2. You're too good for him. 3. You rock. 4. He sucks.

# Pissed-Off Word Search

In a moment of weakness, Samantha hooked up with her ex after she ran into him at a party where he cried for two hours about how much he missed her. Now, after a long night of confessions and Rockin' the Casbah, it turns out Samantha and her ex had very different ideas about what last night meant. She saw it as a new beginning, while he saw it as a stroll down memory lane. Now Samantha's pissed! No amount of cursing and insults is too much for Samantha at this point.

Help Samantha by scouring the Crosswords Word Search and circling as many swear words, curses, names, insults, and angry exclamations as you can find.

| | | | | |
|---|---|---|---|---|
| SHIT | CROCK | POSER | ARSE | BROWNNOSER |
| HALFWIT | GODDAMNSONOFABITCH | DICKWAD | WANKER | MORON |
| CRAP | IHATEYOURFAMILY | DICKHEAD | BASTARD | POMPOUS |
| PISS | SCUMBUCKET | LAZY | LUG | BUGGEROFF |
| GOODRIDDANCE | DOUCHEBAG | DIPSHIT | FUCKHOLE | PUSSY |
| CREEP | BIGMOUTH | CRETAN | LOSER | SELFIMPORTANT |
| FUCK | DICK | PECKERHEAD | BLOCKHEAD | CHICKENSHIT |
| SEEYOUINHELL | LIAR | GEEK | BADINBED | BITEME |
| CRUD | BORING | ANUS | BOOB | HUMORLESS |
| SHITFACE | DICKLESS | ASSKISSER | IDIOT | CHUMP |
| IFAKEDIT | WEINER | HOSEBAG | SELFINVOLVED | |

S E L P S M L D C D K L P B O F E A T R
S D L Y I O S D I C K W A D D O A G O E
E I E L O H K C U F F S E Z I T N T I S
L C H I P E K F N B T V S C Y I U Y D O
R K N M N T M N D A L C W K R D S S I P
O H I A H E I B R O W N N O S E R S C O
M E U F D P L D V O U E B U H K E U K M
U A O R C D E N B L O C K H E A D P L P
H D Y U C H I C K E N S H I T F A C E O
O S E O L F U R K C A E M E T I B R S U
F C E Y L C L M D E H A C A B L H E S S
S U S E L F I M P O R T A N T A L S E P
F M S T P E W R S S O H T U O M G I B M
A B K A I W S E B U G G E R O F F E A R
S U R H E W B S A R S E W A N K E R D R
H C T I B A F O N O S N M A D D O G I G
I K N O G D M L O M H P T O N C R E N A
R E S S I K S S A B G E L A R K I E B D
R T I H S P I D A H R E C U I O E K E K
H O L A G K C O R C S S D C G I N R D A

Word search puzzle key is on page 174.

# The Talk of Shame

Now that Samantha slept with her ex, she has to deal with the repercussions. Not only does that mean grappling with her conscience . . .

. . . she also has to deal with facing her friends.

Help Samantha prepare for the barrage of opinions by anticipating the different responses she's going to get from her friends.

Match the opinions of Samantha's friends in the right column with the bearer of that opinion in the left column on the facing page.

A. Bitter Bonnie

B. Sensitive Cindy

C. Hopeless Hope

D. Powerful Polly

E. Perfect Peg

F. Loose Louise

G. Earthy Erma

H. Heartless Helen

I. Stable Steven

------- 1. I knew you were going to sleep with him again. You have no willpower.

------- 2. It makes sense. We're flowers and we need water. You just want to be careful that the water you're getting isn't infected with all sorts of treacherous chemicals and pesticides.

------- 3. Good for you. Get as much as you can out of him and spit him out when you're done. At least he's good for something.

------- 4. I don't think I like the sound of this; sex without commitment . . . why would anyone do such a thing?

------- 5. Scumbag! Scumbag! Scumbag! Goddamn scumbag!

------- 6. Oh, sweetie, are you okay? It must have been a terribly overwhelming experience; all the hopes and dreams and resentment and rage wrapped into one, fiery expression of love. Come to think of it, that doesn't sound all that bad.

------- 7. You're screwed. It's a no-win situation.

------- 8. Is it the best idea in the world? Probably not. But hey, you're single, he's single, it's Saturday night, and you feel all right. So, what the hell?

------- 9. Did he go downtown, if you know what I mean?

Answers: 1. H; 2. G; 3. D; 4. E; 5. A; 6. B; 7. C; 8. I; 9. F

# Change Machine

We would spend entire Sundays in bed, just laughing and feeding each other cheese and making love again and again. And the next thing you know, it was arguments and resentment.
Maybe he was lactose intolerant.

Samantha's been racking her brain trying to figure out exactly when things went from so good to so bad.

It makes sense that Samantha is having trouble finding the one event that changed the course of her relationship. Rarely, if ever, does just one event exist. Relationships are sneaky; they change little by little without you even realizing it. The next thing you know, you wake up one morning to discover that the person you were dating has grown an extra foot and answers to the name Sven.

Take Samantha through the CHANGE MACHINE below to help illustrate to her the sly and subtle ways in which relationships can go from LOVE to HATE.

Change LOVE into HATE one word at a time by using the clues given.

LOVE

What to do if you're not dead ____________________

What generous people do ____________________

What you did at the office ____________________

A place to do Ecstasy ____________________

Possess stuff ____________________

HATE

Answers: live, give, gave, rave, have

# Homophonia

Hey, it's couples night at the movie theater. You want to go together? They're playing *Endless Love* with Brooke Shields, and we can each get half price.
I think I'm going to skip that one.

Samantha's starting to get wise, and has begun avoiding activities that might impinge her recovery. Samantha has also been seeking out activities that might benefit her recovery. At the top of Samantha's list of productive activities is spending time with her good friend Stable Steven. Stable Steven is loaded with good advice. The only catch is that sometimes Stable Steven gets a little homophonic. Help Samantha decipher Stable Steven's words of wisdom by filling in the blanks in the sentences below. Each sentence contains a pair of homophones (words that mean different things and are spelled differently but sound the same, like "wood" and "would").

1. I was so out of it when my last relationship ended, I remember walking around in a _______ for _______.
2. I felt so _______ for so long, but then in time I came to realize that relationship totally _______.
3. The _______ thing I miss about him at this point is his family's house on the coast of _______. I love lobster.
4. Few things are more daunting than that moment when you _______ that all you can do is say _______! That's it!
5. We _______ these people and everything smells fresh and good and warm. And then one day we wake up and we realize that somehow that smell has evolved into something closer to stale, raw _______.
6. You deserve someone who sees you as a _______ person, not just as a _______.

Answers: 1. daze/days; 2. blue/blew; 3. main/Maine; 4. know/no; 5. meet/meat; 6. whole/hole

# Add-Mitting It was a Mistake

Now that Samantha has had a decent amount of time to put some distance between herself and the relationship and to begin to let the reality of her situation sink in, it's time for her to begin the serious and complicated work of recognizing and analyzing the relationship's flaws.

Samantha is surrounded by clues that will help her gain greater understanding of her current circumstances. Add up the clues below so that Samantha can begin to gain the much-needed perspective that she so desperately desires.

**A g +** 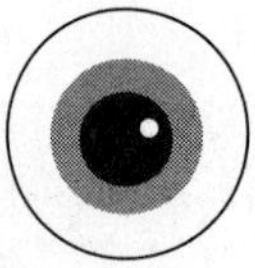 **+**  **+**  **(– nake) + T**

**+**  **(– P) + P +** 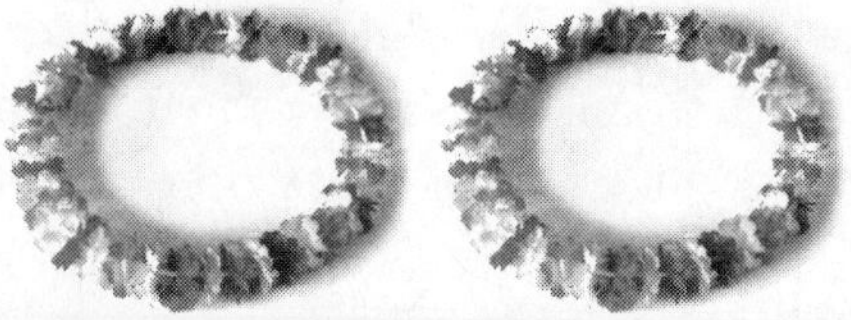 **with**

**"Action" + "Fig" + "yours" is**  **+ red +**

**E + 4 (+ M (or Mmm) + Carriage – C.**

---

Answer: A guy who still plays with action figures is not ready for marriage.

# The Right words at the Right Time

Samantha's ex has called her up at 1:45 in the morning "just to say hi." Samantha has neither the energy nor the desire to get into a big thing with her ex right now. It's too late, she's too tired, and she's not even sure if what's happening is even real or merely a dream. Under the circumstances, there's only one thing Samantha needs to say to her ex. Something that will convey all of those sentiments quickly and concisely . . .

GO FUCK YOURSELF!

Considering the hour and Samantha's dazed state, just managing to get those simple three words out in order will be much more difficult than it seems. Dancing around Samantha's head are all three words dozens of times over, but if you look closer, you'll notice how scrambled the words really are. In fact, there is only one spot in Samantha's head where Go Fuck Yourself appears in order. Help Samantha find it, and then circle it so that Samantha can tell her ex off right.

GO YOURSELF FUCK GO
FUCK FUCK YOURSELF FUCK GO FUCK GO
FUCK FUCK YOURSELF YOURSELF FUCK GO
YOURSELF FUCK YOURSELF FUCK GO FUCK GO FUCK
GO YOURSELF FUCK FUCK FUCK YOURSELF YOURSELF
YOURSELF GO YOURSELF FUCK GO GO YOURSELF FUCK GO
FUCK FUCK GO GO FUCK GO FUCK YOURSELF FUCK FUCK
YOURSELF GO GO FUCK GO YOURSELF FUCK YOURSELF
FUCK YOURSELF GO GO FUCK FUCK YOURSELF
FUCK GO YOURSELF FUCK YOURSELF
YOURSELF FUCK GO GO FUCK GO
YOURSELF FUCK FUCK FUCK YOURSELF
GO YOURSELF FUCK GO FUCK GO
YOURSELF GO FUCK GO FUCK FUCK
FUCK YOURSELF YOURSELF FUCK GO
YOURSELF FUCK YOURSELF FUCK
GO FUCK GO FUCK GO
YOURSELF GO FUCK FUCK
FUCK YOURSELF
FUCK GO

# Value Balls

How are we ever going to have a healthy relationship if you can't be honest with me?
I can be honest with you.
I mean all the time.
Wow. That's a lot.

One of the problems that Samantha and her ex faced was that their relationship lacked some of the basic values that should be at the heart of any successful partnership. Throughout the relationship, there were voids that prevented Samantha and her ex from reaching these ideals. Help Samantha write the missing letters into the value balls below in order to discover the hidden value written in each line. Once you're done, read the letters inside the value balls from top to bottom to discover an extra-special something that would've helped Samantha's self-esteem and temperament tremendously throughout the relationship.

| | | | | | | | | | | | |
|---|---|---|---|---|---|---|---|---|---|---|---|
| A | F | F | E | | T | I | O | N | S | | |
| T | R | | S | T | | | | | | | |
| H | O | | E | S | T | Y | | | | | |
| A | C | C | E | P | T | A | | C | E | | |
| F | A | | T | H | | | | | | | |
| | O | V | E | | | | | | | | |
| C | O | M | M | | T | M | E | N | T | | |
| S | E | | S | E | O | F | H | U | M | O | R |
| | O | O | O | D | N | E | S | S | | | |
| S | | P | P | O | R | T | | | | | |
| O | P | E | N | N | E | | S | | | | |

Answers: affections, trust, honesty, acceptance, faith, love, commitment, sense of humor, goodness, support, openness. Extra-Special Bonus: Cunnilingus

# Last Things First!

Samantha spent most of her relationship putting herself last. Old habits die hard.

Samantha needs to start learning how to put herself first. Her habit of putting first things last has gotten so bad that it's crept into her speech. Below are some words that Samantha would like to be able to say, but every time she tries, the first letter of each word ends up at the word's end. Help Samantha start to switch things around by taking the last letter from each word and putting it back in front where it belongs.

I wish I had one!
Man, this ice cream cone is delicious.
You can have mine if you want. I don't mind—really!

**Noughe fo hist onsensen, 'mi hrought layingp econds**

**iddlef. heret si a otl hatt I antw nda m'I oingg**

**ot etg ti. Ustj ryt ot tops em. I ared ouy.**

**hat'st ightr, ouy eardh em. I eserved ot eb reatedt**

**ightr. I eserved ot od hatw I antw ot. os, teps**

**sidea fi ouy an'tc etg ithw hatt, ecauseb I otg**

**on imet ot arryc oury ssa.**

Answer: Enough of this nonsense, I'm through playing second fiddle. There is a lot that I want and I'm going to get it. Just try to stop me. I dare you. That's right, you heard me. I deserve to be treated right. I deserve to do what I want to. So, step aside if you can't get with that, because I got no time to carry your ass.

# The Cocksucker Crutch: An In-Depth Look

Samantha has recently gotten into the dangerous habit of avoiding any greater contemplation of her relationship by relying on the Cocksucker Crutch.

I heard he's buying a motorcycle.
Figures. Cocksucker.
So, do you still think about him?
That cocksucker? Please.
Do you know what time it is?
I can't believe that cocksucker.

As much as Samantha would like to keep counting on the Cocksucker Crutch, it's going to wear out sooner or later. Luckily, there's a wealth of other words hiding in the word "Cocksucker" that will help add variety to Samantha's repertoire and rescue her from her cocksucker rut.

Help Samantha find as many words as she can hidden in the word

**C-O-C-K-S-U-C-K-E-R**

Answers: Cock, Suck, Sucker, Curse, Sour, Ruse, Rouse, Crock, Cure, User, Uck (not really a word, but very appropriate), Rock, Rocks, Coke, Sock, Cork, Cur (as in a nasty mutt or a cruel, spineless or unlikable individual)

# Cross Check!

As Samantha gets more and more distance between herself and her relationship, she's beginning to wonder what it was that attracted her to her ex in the first place.

Check it out!
I can fart on
command.

Using the meticulous *Dumped: Fun and Games Activity Book* process of elimination, help Samantha cross off those qualities that her ex did not possess, allowing her to recognize what it was about him that drew her in the first place.

Cross off any words with two of the same letters in a row.
Cross off any words that begin with G.
Cross off any words that end with L.
Cross off any words with three or more syllables.
Cross off any word whose first syllable means to commit an act of transgression in opposition to a moral/ethical code.

**Loyal Generous Thoughtful Attentive Positive**

**Affectionate Giving Deep Strong-willed Charming Sincere**

**Truthful Cute Helpful Gentle Considerate Compassionate**

**Supportive Encouraging Sensitive Funny**

Answer: ~~Loyal~~ ~~Generous~~ ~~Thoughtful~~ ~~Attentive~~ ~~Positive~~ ~~Affectionate~~ ~~Giving~~ ~~Deep~~ ~~Strong-willed~~ ~~Charming~~ ~~Sincere~~ ~~Truthful~~ Cute ~~Helpful~~ ~~Gentle~~ ~~Considerate~~ ~~Compassionate~~ ~~Supportive~~ ~~Encouraging~~ ~~Sensitive~~ Funny

# Dumped Delectables

Samantha's just been through a long night of ex-boyfriend nonsense.

Samantha's earned herself a post-insanity treat and nothing says, "What the fuck was that all about?" better than the . . .

I did not say that.
Yes, you did.
No, I didn't.
Yes, you did.
No, I didn't.
Nothing like good, sound, intelligent discourse.

**PEPPERIDGE Tri-Pint Fun-A-Palooza!**

Here's how you do it! First you're going to need:

- Three pints of your favorite ice cream. Samantha's favorites are Chocolate Chip Cookie Dough, Coffee, and something real chocolatey like New York Super Fudge Chunk or Chocolate Fudge Brownie.
- Box of Pepperidge Farm chocolate chunk cookies. Preferably not soft baked. Nothing against soft baked, but they just don't provide the necessary textural contrast of the Original Crunchy Pepperidge Farm cookies, which include Chesapeake, Nantucket, and Sausalito.
- Bowl
- Hammer
- Spoon

DIRECTIONS:

1. Empty contents of cookie bag into bowl.
2. Smash cookies with hammer.
3. Empty contents of three ice cream pints into bowl.
4. Stir.
5. Enjoy.

# The Fact of the Matter

Samantha's been doing a terrific job recently of evaluating her relationship.

There's one issue, however, that all of Samantha's fantastic analyses has not unearthed yet. At the very center of Samantha's ex's core lay a gnawing lack of confidence, for which he's constantly overcompensating. His need to control, dominate, and belittle can all be traced back to this one quality.

Help Samantha find out the cause of his neurosis by circling all of the letters in the chart that are not N, L, Z, A, I, E, P, S, or M. Read the remaining letters to discover the answer.

| | | | | | | | | |
|---|---|---|---|---|---|---|---|---|
| B | Y | S | C | K | F | H | M | J |
| A | T | V | G | L | X | O | L | R |
| D | O | P | Q | T | E | N | D | C |
| R | I | T | S | X | F | C | S | D |
| I | B | O | Z | G | E | T | Y | T |

Answer: Small penis size

# Samantha's Breakup-Joke Corner

Why did my ex-boyfriend cross the road?
*Answer:* Because he's a selfish prick who does whatever the hell he wants.

How many ex-boyfriends does it take to screw in a light bulb?
*Answer:* All of them. They'll screw anything.

What do my ex-boyfriend and Oscar Meyer have in common?
*Answer:* They both like to sing songs about their overrated wieners.

What's the difference between my boyfriend and toothpaste?
*Answer:* Toothpaste cleans your teeth. My ex is a dick.

How do you know when your ex-boyfriend's been in your refrigerator?
*Answer:* When you don't have any goddamn food.

Ex-Boyfriend: Knock! Knock!
Samantha: Who's there?
Ex-Boyfriend: Your ex-boyfriend.
Samantha: Go away!
Ex-Boyfriend: You're supposed to say, "Your ex-boyfriend who?"
Samantha: Go away!

# Going Up?: Volume 2

Samantha's been feeling a little low lately.

Looks like it's time for another ride in the . . . uplift elevators!

This time Samantha gets to ride in the "Ch" Elevator! The Ch Elevator has three floors that Samantha can visit. All of the other floors would only make Samantha feel worse. Take a look at all of the buttons in the Ch Elevator and color in the ones that would be best for Samantha.

## Ch-

| | | | |
|---|---|---|---|
| afing | eated | icken | unky |
| agrined | eerful | intzy | inless |
| alky | ewed up | erished | oice |
| allenged | illy | ubby | opped up and spit out |

Answers: Cheerful, Cherished, Choice

# Conjugate This!!!

Samantha's ex has shown up at her place drunk.

You reek.
It's my passion for you.
I'd recognize that stale, unsavory smell anywhere.

Samantha's ex wants to spend the night.

Samantha has many things she'd like to say to her ex and they all involve the word "fuck." Help Samantha find the right conjugations of the word fuck for each of the following sentences.

Fill in the blank with the appropriate option: Fuck, Fucking, Fucker, Fucked

1. You've got to be ____________ kidding me! You mother ____________!
2. Who the ____________ do you think you are?! You're so ____________ up!
3. ____________ you! I can't ____________ believe you!
4. Go ____________ yourself!!! This whole thing is so ____________!
5. You ____________ ____________! Argh! ____________ you! ____________ you!

Answers: 1. Fucking/fucker; 2. Fuck/fucked; 3. Fuck/fucking; 4. Fuck/fucked; 5. Fucking/fuck/fuck/fuck

# Three Strikes, You're Out

This is the third time in a week that Samantha's ex has either called or shown up on Samantha's doorstep between the hours of 12:41 A.M. and 3:12 A.M.

Maybe he just lost his keys and didn't know where else to go.
You need keys to get back into hell?

Samantha's ex has struck out. Help Samantha make that clear to him by solving the three-strikes puzzle. Each word below has one extra letter in it that appears three times. Strike a line through the extra three letters in order to help Samantha find the right words to say to her ex.

**BGBOB LHLOMLE, VYOVVU LOCSCERC.**

**YHOHURH KMKOMKMY'S SCASLSLING NYONUN**

__________ __________, __________ __________.

__________ __________ __________ __________.

Answer: Go home, you loser. Your mommy's calling you.

# Heart of Glass!

She should probably avoid Whitney Houston's "I Will Always Love You."
And "Hopelessly Devoted to You," from the *Grease* soundtrack.
God, I love that movie. That Rizzo is such a badass.

Samantha just hit a landmark in her development! "I was sitting in my living room eating a Sara Lee Original Cherry Cheesecake and listening to Air Supply's 'I'm All Out of Love, I'm So Lost Without You,' when it hit me like a ton of bricks—Air Supply is sucking the life out of me!"

Samantha's willingness to cast aside the Australian soft-rock superstars' 1980 chart-topping international mega-hit single about unrequited love is a giant leap forward in her recovery process. The next step in Samantha's development is to find her some new music. Help Samantha find the music that she needs to continue her journey down the path to resurrection.

1. For starters, Samantha would like the classic heartbreak anthem, "Heart of Glass." Who is it by?
   - A. Green Day
   - B. Pink
   - C. The Moody Blues
   - D. Blondie

2. Samantha wants a song by Cher. Which song is a Cher classic?
   A. "Believe"
   B. "Imagine"
   C. "Jump"
   D. "Kiss"

3. Samantha would like the song "Bye, Bye, Bye." Who is it by?
   A. Backstreet Boys
   B. *N Sync
   C. Credence Clearwater Revival

4. Samantha would definitely like a song by Tom Petty and the Heartbreakers. Which should she get?
   A. "Don't Come Around Here No More"
   B. "Here Comes My Girl"

5. Samantha would like to get the song, "Hit the Road, Jack." Who is it by?
   A. Barry Gibb
   B. Chuck Berry
   C. Ray Charles
   D. Ray Romano

6. Samantha's been thinking a lot about her destiny, so naturally, she'd like a song by Destiny's Child. Which would you suggest?
   A. "Survivor"
   B. "Bootylicious"

7. Samantha would like some guidance from one of the first ladies of song, Miss Diana Ross. What song best suits her current needs?
   A. "Your Love Is So Good for Me"
   B. "I'm Coming Out"
   C. "If We Hold on Together"
   D. "Baby I Love Your Way"

8. No one had more to say on the subject of love than the Chairman of the Board himself, Ole Blue Eyes, Frank Sinatra. What song should old Frankie serenade Samantha with?
   A. "Polka Dots and Moonbeams"
   B. "My Way"

9. Finally, Samantha would like to get a song by the multiplatinum, Grammy Award–winning, original badass vixen of vocals, Pat Benatar. Which song should Samantha get?
   A. "Hit Me with Your Best Shot"
   B. "Fire and Ice"
   C. "I Want Out"
   D. "Heartbreaker"
   E. "All Fired Up"
   F. "You Better Run"
   G. "No You Don't"
   H. "Little Too Late"
   I. "Have It All"
   J. "Love Is a Battlefield"

Answers: 1. D; 2. A; 3. B; 4. A; 5. C; 6. BOTH; 7. B; 8. B; 9. ALL! ALL! ALL!

# Going Pro

Samantha spent a great deal of the last seven-and-a-half years basing her decisions on the wants and whims of her ex. Now that Samantha's single, the time has come for her to learn how to be PROactive again. Samantha's surrounded by "pros" everywhere she looks, she just needs a little help making sense of them. Help her define these pros by matching up the suffixes on the bottom of the page with the appropriate sentences.

1. Enough of this sitting around and waiting to feel better; it's time I pro__________ the depths of my experience in order to come up with some legitimate answers.

2. No more pro__________ with caution. I'm getting this show on the road.

3. I know I have a pro__________ to sit back and take things as they come, but I'm learning how to go out and pro__________ the things that I need.

4. Enough pro__________; it's time to get down to business.

5. What was I thinking? The idea of pro__________ to him is the national football league adding an expansion team.

6. I kept waiting for him to pro__________ that ring, pro__________ his love, and then pro__________. Shit! Excuse my pro__________.

7. I passed up some pro__________ people to be with his ass. First, there was my sociology pro__________, then there was a successful computer pro__________, and even a chief pro__________ from the district attorney's office.

8. It's enough to make me pro__________ vomit.

**Suffixes**

| | | | |
|---|---|---|---|
| -duce | -minent | -clivity | -crastinating |
| -ceeding | -secutor | -fess | -fanity |
| -grammer | -pose | -fessor | -cure |
| -jectile | | | |

Answers: proceeding, proclivity, procure, procrastinating, produce, profess, propose, profanity, prominent, professor, programmer, prosecutor, projectile

# web of Lies

Samantha has always had trouble knowing when to believe her ex. It's no different now that they're broken up. Help Samantha escape her ex's WEB OF LIES once and for all. Start in the middle of the web and find your way to the outside by slipping through the openings in it.

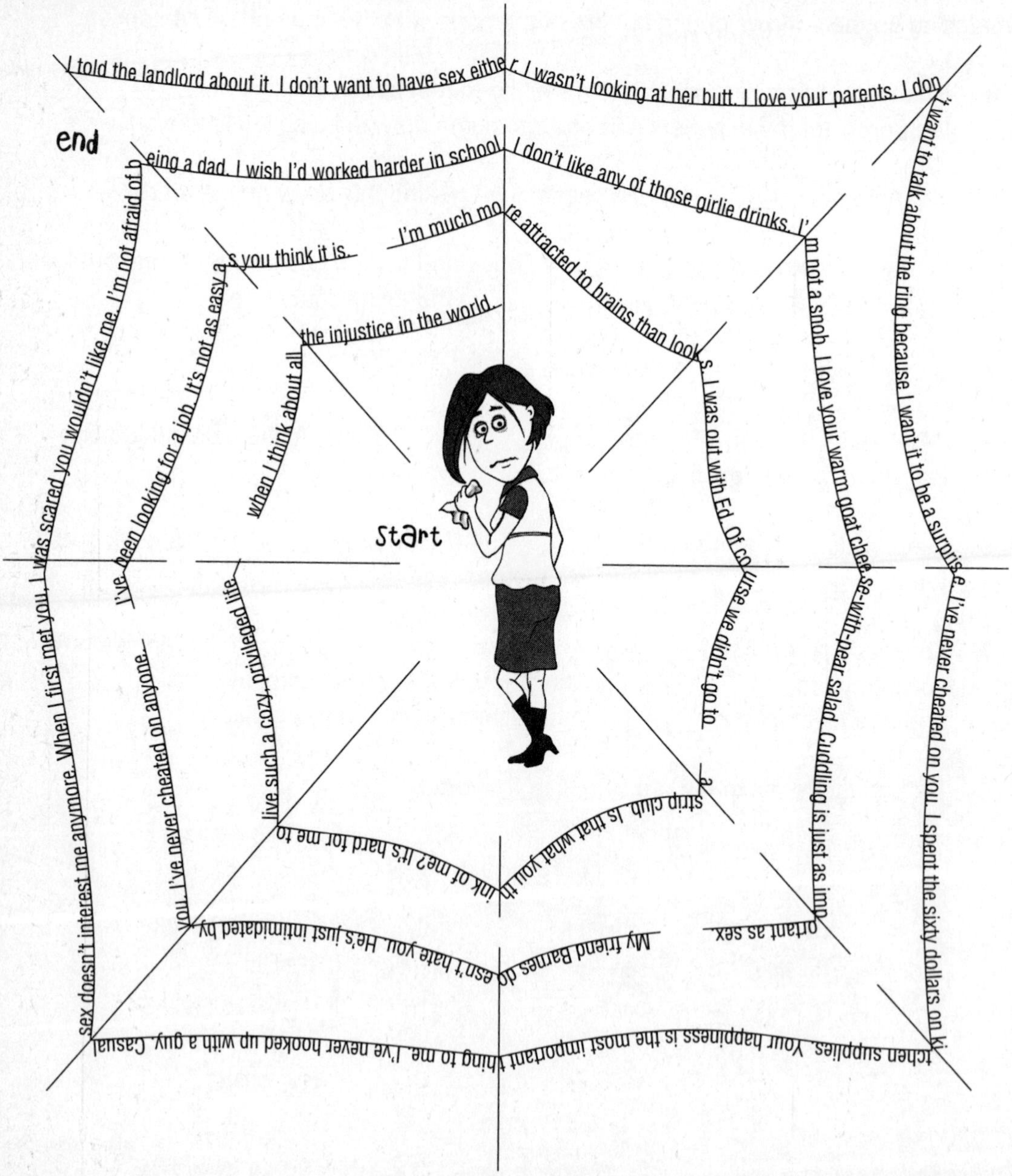
end
Start
I told the landlord about it. I don't want to have sex either. I wasn't looking at her butt. I love your parents. I don't want to talk about the ring because I want it to be a surprise. I've never cheated on you. I spent the sixty dollars on kitchen supplies. Your happiness is the most important thing to me. I've never hooked up with a guy. Casual sex doesn't interest me anymore. When I first met you, I was scared you wouldn't like me. I'm not afraid of being a dad. I wish I'd worked harder in school
I don't like any of those girlie drinks. I'm not a snob. I love your warm goat cheese-with-pear salad. Cuddling is just as important as sex.
My friend Barnes doesn't hate you. He's just intimidated by you. I've never cheated on anyone.
I've been looking for a job. It's not as easy as you think it is.
I'm much more attracted to brains than looks. I was out with Ed. Of course we didn't go to a strip club. Is that what you think of me? It's hard for me to live such a cozy, privileged life when I think about all the injustice in the world.

# Baby Steps

Samantha's frustrated. She's scared that she's going to feel miserable for the rest of her life.

The thing Samantha doesn't realize is that those good feelings that she's longing to feel aren't nearly as far away as they seem.

I know exactly how you feel. I was involved with this one bison for four years. She was the sweetest little prairie cow you ever saw. But you get over these things. I did. You should see the ox I'm dating now! Whoo, Doggie!

Below are 12 pairs of words. Each pair has a Before/Gloom word and an After/Bloom word. Like "gloom" and "bloom," both words share every letter but one. Help Samantha see that the good feelings are just one step away by filling in the missing letters and identifying the Before/After Gloom terms.

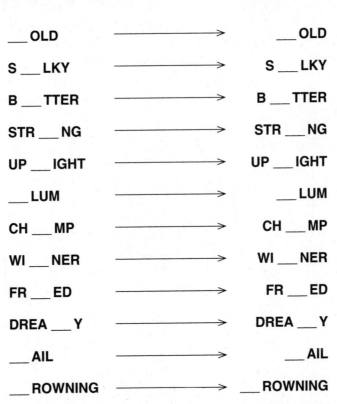

| | | |
|---|---|---|
| ___ OLD | ⟶ | ___ OLD |
| S ___ LKY | ⟶ | S ___ LKY |
| B ___ TTER | ⟶ | B ___ TTER |
| STR ___ NG | ⟶ | STR ___ NG |
| UP ___ IGHT | ⟶ | UP ___ IGHT |
| ___ LUM | ⟶ | ___ LUM |
| CH ___ MP | ⟶ | CH ___ MP |
| WI ___ NER | ⟶ | WI ___ NER |
| FR ___ ED | ⟶ | FR ___ ED |
| DREA ___ Y | ⟶ | DREA ___ Y |
| ___ AIL | ⟶ | ___ AIL |
| ___ ROWNING | ⟶ | ___ ROWNING |

Answers: cold/bold, sulky/silky, bitter/better, strung/strong, uptight/upright, glum/plum, chump/champ, wiener/winner, fried/freed, dreary/dreamy, fail/sail, drowning/crowning

# Boxing Match!

**Two-Person Game! Twice the Dumped Fun!**

Samantha's ex has come over to move his stuff out!

Samantha, as usual, has chosen to take the high road, and agreed to help him pack up his stuff. Samantha and her ex work quickly and efficiently in silence, but, as always, a battle is secretly taking place between them.

**Who can pack up the most boxes?**

**This can be a fun game to play with your ex!**

Find another player. Choose one of you to be Samantha and one of you to be her ex. Alternate turns connecting the dots with a single line. Whenever someone draws a line that creates a box, that person puts the initials of the person they're playing for on the label in the box—"S" for Samantha and "E" for Ex. The player that ends up with the most boxes wins.

**Here's a chance to do it with boxes of kitchen utensils.**

## Now try it with books.

**How 'bout a bunch of boxes of random crap?**

# Spell It Out!

Samantha was going to dump her boyfriend seven months ago, but she decided not to after he was diagnosed with irritable bowel syndrome. Once he had his condition under control, Samantha's ex dumped Samantha. Now, he's back at her door at 3:00 A.M., claiming to want her back.

I need you. I've always needed you.
Except for those times when you didn't need me, and you dumped me.

This is a critical moment for Samantha. She can keep riding the evil breakup merry-go-round with her boyfriend or she can make it clear to him that she's sick of the nonsense and ready to move on. Help Samantha spell it out for her boyfriend that she's not coming back. Fill in the words that match the symbols to create the phrases.

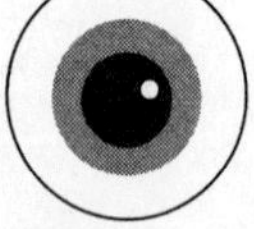 +  +  +  + **"But"** +

1
May

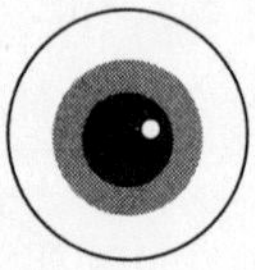 **+ M +**  **+ "Crazy." +**  **+ U.**

------------------------------------------------------------

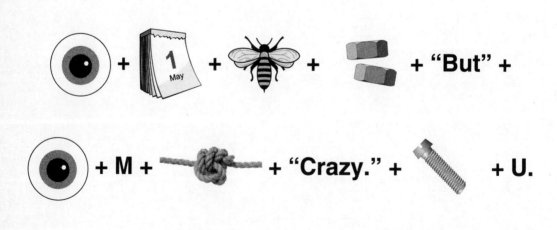

Answer: I may be nuts but I'm not crazy. Screw you.

# Fact or Friction

Samantha's ex isn't giving up! For the millionth time, Samantha's ex is telling her, "This time it'll be different; I'll never take you for granted again." How can Samantha gauge his sincerity, you may ask.

How can
Samantha gauge
his sincerity?

*By looking at the facts.* Help Samantha get a read on her ex by trying to see if you can tell which things Samantha's ex is saying are facts and which things are only going to lead to greater conflict or friction. Write "fact" or "friction" on the lines below.

1. There's nothing I wouldn't do for you. ________
2. I may be stupid, but I'm not cruel. ________
3. You don't even care what I have to say. ________
4. You think I wake up in the morning and ask myself, "How can I mess with Samantha today?" ________
5. I'm tired of playing games. ________
6. All I wanna do is kiss you right now. ________
7. I may have kept some things from you, but I never outright lied to you. ________
8. I admit it—I've been an asshole! ________

Answers: 1. Friction: If that were true they'd be married with three children by now. 2. Friction: He's stupid and cruel. 3. Fact. 4. Fact: She does think that. 5. Friction: If he were tired of playing games, he wouldn't still be playing them. 6. Friction: He also wants a blowjob. 7. Friction: That's a lie H. Fact!

# Are you High?

Despite all of her reasons for not getting back together with her ex, Samantha has actually started considering getting back together with him!

I don't know . . . maybe he's changed.
Say what?!
What kind of crack have you been smoking?

All those months of meaningful introspection seem to have flown out the door with the arrival of the news of Samantha's sister's engagement.

Samantha needs to gain some perspective fast, before she does something she might really regret, and nothing says perspective better than a rousing game of Are You High?

Help Samantha gather her bearings by reading the statements below and trying to figure out if the numbers are High, Low, or Right on the Money.

Write "High, Low, or Right on the Money" on the appropriate lines.

1. On one particularly passionate evening of lovemaking, Samantha climaxed thirty-one times while engaged in intercourse with her ex. __________

2. Samantha and her ex have broken up a total of sixteen times. __________

3. Samantha's ex has assured Samantha that he had begun engagement ring shopping nine times. __________

4. On their last vacation, while in Playa Blanca, Mexico, Samantha's ex beat his own record by drinking nineteen margaritas on their last night there. __________

5. Before getting dumped by her ex, Samantha gave him forty-six "second chances" to shape up or ship out. __________

6. Samantha's most blunt and uncompromising friend, Vicki Tetley, told Samantha to break up with her ex 2,586 times. __________

7. The subject of having kids and raising a family was discussed in earnest only four times between Samantha and her ex. __________

8. Samantha's ex still owes her $612 for rent past due, some utilities, and a Weezer CD that she lent him the money for. __________

Answers: 1. High: Her record is twice . . . which happened once. 2. Right on the money: They've broken up sixteen times, including a record three times on Samantha's birthday two years ago. 3. High: He only told her that seven times. 4. Right on the money: He topped this achievement by frequently shitting his pants over the next eight hours. 5. Low: While no official number is available, Samantha gave her ex at least seventy-one "second chances." 6. High: This is a gross exaggeration. Vicki only told Samantha to dump her ex 1,709 times. 7. High: It was never discussed. Every time Samantha tried to discuss it, her ex assured her that he wanted to have the conversation, but only when they could be guaranteed to have the proper amount of time to discuss it properly, which is a completely valid point, although less so when he made it while playing X-Box or watching reruns of *The Real World/Road Rules Challenge* on MTV. 8. Low! Low! Low!: Samantha's ex owes her close to three Gs.

# Got a Nice "Ing" to It

Samantha's ex just can't deal with the fact that Samantha's rejecting him.

Samantha's ex is pulling out all the stops. What Samantha's ex is doing is trying to throw Samantha off by hitting her with a barrage of "ING": doING; amazING; nothING; havING; dealING; movING; meanING; feelINGs; reelING.

Samantha is no longer thrown off that easily. She can play the ING game and she can do it in rhyme. She just needs a little help from you at the end of the lines, which all happen to end in "ING." Use the letters at the side of the page to attach to the INGs.

Your breakup from me really did ___________.

But I'm on the mend now, I'm on an ______________.

It's like winter has passed and I'm onto ____________.

I can see the trees blooming and hear the birds _________.

So, stop wasting your time and stop doing your ___________.

I'm no longer your princess and you're not my ________.

I'm done needing you, don't expect me to __________.

I'm going to go out and have me a ___________.

S
CL
SPR
TH
FL
ST
K
UPSW

Answers: sting, upswing, spring, sing, thing, king, cling, fling

# wisdom of the Ages

Samantha's taken a trip to see her favorite person and most trusted advisor—her grandmother. Unfortunately, Grandma's getting on in years and her mind isn't quite as sharp as it once was.

G ilmu rfyr.
That's a poodle, Grandma, not a comb.

Still, even in her current state, Grandma has great insights to offer once one can decipher what it is that she's trying to say. One need only take a step back, two in fact, to get to the true meaning of Grandma's words. Replace every letter below with the letter in the alphabet that comes exactly two letters after it to discover what it is that Granny has to say to Samantha about her misfortune.

For example, Grandma's jumbled response to Samantha above is, "I know that."
*Note:* for letters at the end of the alphabet, go back to the beginning of the alphabet.

_ _____ _____ ____ ___.

**G LCTCP JGICB RFYR ZMW.**

__ ___ _ ____ ____, ___ __ ______

**FC FYB Y LGAC PSKN, ZSR FC QCCKCB**

____ _ ______.

**JGIC Y BMSAFC.**

Answer: I never liked that boy. He had a nice rump, but he seemed like a douche.

# Rhymes and Reasons

Samantha's ex is starting to take Samantha's rejection personally. He claims there's no rhyme or reason for Samantha rejecting him. But Samantha's got plenty of rhymes and reasons; all she needs is a little assistance with the endings. Help Samantha tell her ex off by completing the rhyming phrases below.

1. I'm so done with you; you're no good for my health
   If you're that hard up fellah, you should go fuck __________.
2. I've told you before that I won't take your calls
   Try to reach me again and I'll rip off your __________.
3. Everything's changed, it cannot be the same
   This entire discussion is so totally __________.
4. You show up all cocky and acting all cool
   I'm done swooning for you and you won't see me __________.
5. You exclaim that you need me, without me you're dead
   But I know you too well you just want to get __________.
6. How can you come here after all that you've done?
   Have you really no shame? My God, you're pond __________.
7. It was your choice to end it, so the blame is all yours
   Although it's fun seeing you, begging on all __________.
8. I feel good, I feel strong, I'm defeating the ache
   By the way, those orgasms . . . most of them were __________.
9. You left me so lost, wondering where did my will go
   But I've got a new love he's a vibrating __________.
10. You can show yourself out, you have done it before
    Be sure that your ass don't get smacked by the __________.

Answers: 1. yourself; 2. balls; 3. lame; 4. drool; 5. head; 6. scum; 7. fours; 8. fake; 9. dildo; 10. door

# Dear John Letters

Samantha's decided the best way to proceed with her ex is to write him a letter rather than have any more contact with him in person or over the phone.

That's how we used to do it in the days of yore.

For some reason, Samantha's typewriter refuses to print out the third letter of every word, making it difficult to decipher some very critical words. It just so happens that every letter in the alphabet is left out once. Use the alphabet chart to help Samantha fill in all the missing letters in her letter.

**A B C D E F G H I J K L M N O P Q R S T U V W X Y Z**

| | | | |
|---|---|---|---|
| Su__fering | Ap__reciate | Ro__ot | Te__uila |
| Bo__ed | Be__ch | Dr__wning | Li__id |
| Fi__hting | Ex__austed | Sl__my | En__ |
| Fa__igued | De__ected | Ac__used | Me__ories |
| No__sensical | St__mied | Lo__down | Pe__ce |
| Us__less | Pi__sed | Se__ist | |
| Bi__arre | Gr__eling | Jo__e | |

Answers: SuFfering, BoRed, FiGhting, FaTigued, NoNsensical, UsEless, BiZarre, ApPreciate, BeLch, ExHausted, DeJected, StYmied, PiSsed, GrUeling, RoBot, DrOwning, SlImy, AcCused, LoWdown, SeXist, JoKe, TeQuila, LiVid, EnD, MeMories, PeAce

# The Difference Between GOOD and POO

At this point, Samantha should be starting to feel relief more than anything else.

The unfortunate reality is that Samantha's head is still spinning so fast that it's hard for her to differentiate the positive from the negative. The complex nature of her mother tongue, English, doesn't help to simplify things for her either.

Take, for instance, the classic double-letter combination of "OO." So strong and self-assured, "OO" can sOOthe and "OO" can wOO. Placed in the wrong context, however, "OO" just as easily turns to glOOm, which explains why Samantha's feeling more than a little cuckOO these days.

Help Samantha fill in the missing letters around the "OO"s in the words below. This will remind her that although they may share some of the same letters, there is a huge difference between GOOD and POO.

1. Samantha deserves to be in a relationship where she can flourish and __ __OO__, which is never going to happen in a relationship that was obviously __OO__ __ __ from the beginning.

2. Samantha needs a hot-__ __OO__ __ __ man, one who's thoughtful, considerate, and confident in his __ __ __ __OO__. For Christ's sake, in seven-and-a-half years her ex never once even left the toilet seat down for her in the __ __ __ __ __OO__.

3. Samantha ought to have a man who's able to make her __ __OO__ with just one touch of a finger or the glance of an eye. What she doesn't need is another penniless __ OO__ __ __ __ who's always hemming and hawing and __ __ __ __ __ __OO__ __ __ __ around.

4. It would also be nice to meet a guy who's concerned with more than his own little __OO__ __.

5. Samantha should've given her ex the __OO__ ages ago when he had the nerve to ask her to get a __OO__ job. For the record, Samantha's breasts are perfect just as they are, thank you very much!

6. A critical sign that something was terribly lacking in Samantha's relationship was when she found herself __ __OO__ __ __ __ while watching __ __ __ OO__ __ making __ __OO__ __ __ on the Discovery Channel. If that doesn't tell you the __ __ __ __ __ __OO__ is over, what does?

7. Sure, no relationship is perfect, but for the most part they should run __ __ OO__ __ __ __.

8. The relationship ran its course, and like __ __ __ __ __OO__ __ __ pasta, by the end was nothing but a flimsy, mushy, unappetizing version of its former self.

Answers: 1. bloom/doomed; 2. blooded/manhood/bathroom; 3. swoon/moocher/pussyfooting; 4. woody; 5. boot/boob; 6. drooling/baboons/whoopie/honeymoon; 7. smoothly; 8. overcooked

# Ass + hole =

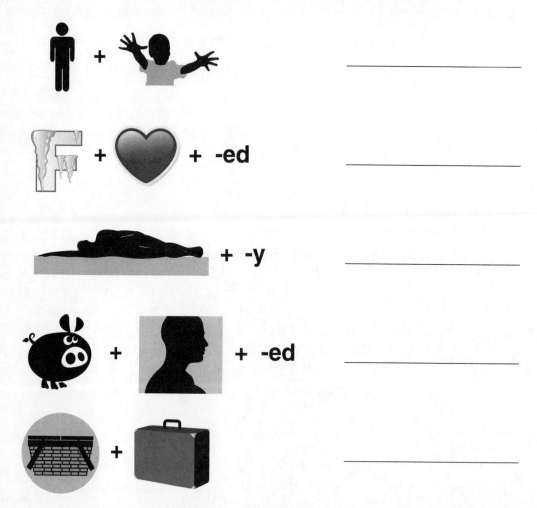

Samantha is getting very confused. It wasn't that long ago that her ex didn't seem to want to have anything to do with her. Now, suddenly, he can't seem to live without her.

The whole experience is quite baffling to Samantha. One thing is clear: She mustn't let go of her ability to identify facts and connect them to other facts in order to come to well-informed conclusions.

Below are 10 pairs of drawings. Identify each pair of drawings. Then put the two words from the drawings together to create another word to describe Samantha's ex.

 +  ____________________

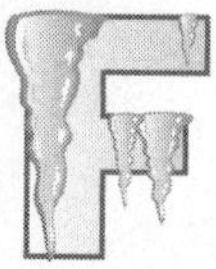 +  + -ed ____________________

 + -y ____________________

 + 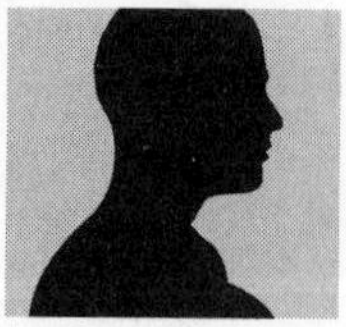 + -ed ____________________

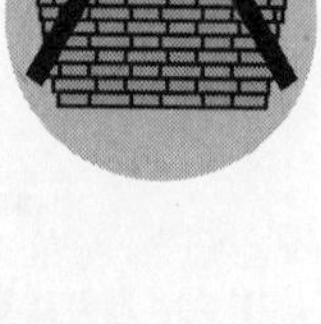 +  ____________________

Answers: Man child, Cold-hearted, Slothful, Pig-headed, Basket case

# Going Up?: Volume 3

Samantha's doing so great that she's earned herself another ride on the uplift elevators!

This time, Samantha gets to ride in the "Su" Elevator! The Su Elevator has five floors that Samantha can visit. Take a look at all of the buttons in the Su Elevator and color in the ones that would be best for Samantha.

## Su-

| | | | | |
|---|---|---|---|---|
| lky | ccessful | cky | spicious | percilious |
| bservient | spect | perstitious | llen | icidal |
| percharged | rly | ndried | bstandard | pine |
| ffering | per-duper | nken | sceptible | mmarized |
| bpar | lfurous | blime | preme | ffocated |

Answers: Supercharged, Successful, Super-duper, Sublime, Supreme

# Blessings in Disguise

Samantha's YOUNGER sister and her boyfriend have just announced their engagement at the family's Thanksgiving dinner. This news has rendered Samantha utterly speechless.

Uh . . . uh . . . uh . . .

She literally can't find the appropriate words to say. All that keeps popping into her head is, "I'm going to kill myself. I'm going to kill myself. I'm going to kill myself."

Not that Samantha isn't happy for her sister; she is. Or at least she will be eventually (hopefully). But right now, Samantha can't stop thinking about the fact that her YOUNGER sister will be getting married before her, and that makes her want to kill herself.

Fortunately, the right words haven't gone too far—they're all in the word search below. Help Samantha give her sister her blessing by finding the words hidden in the puzzle below. Be careful, though; there are some wrong words hidden in there, too, and you wouldn't want Samantha to accidentally blurt those out to her sister. Cross the bad words out, just to be safe.

| | | | | | | | | | | | | | |
|---|---|---|---|---|---|---|---|---|---|---|---|---|---|
| S | E | I | I | O | C | E | P | B | A | R | T | L | G |
| N | M | T | N | T | E | R | R | I | F | I | C | N | E |
| O | S | A | F | S | S | I | P | N | I | E | F | N | R |
| I | C | S | C | C | L | G | O | D | D | A | M | N | A |
| T | N | E | L | L | E | C | X | E | N | T | C | P | I |
| A | R | B | I | T | C | H | K | T | L | T | E | M | C |
| L | L | A | I | S | P | P | A | E | E | A | F | T | C |
| U | N | S | U | G | H | S | T | U | E | F | A | G | K |
| T | F | P | T | R | T | P | H | T | T | E | P | F | B |
| A | E | U | P | I | G | A | C | I | B | M | I | T | T |
| R | E | K | C | U | F | R | E | H | T | O | M | M | T |
| G | S | I | N | K | G | C | K | R | X | C | F | K | E |
| N | T | O | I | N | A | A | K | D | G | S | O | L | C |
| O | I | I | N | A | I | I | T | R | O | N | M | H | O |
| C | T | C | R | S | C | C | O | R | R | S | O | I | C |

| | |
|---|---|
| CONGRATULATIONS | CRAP |
| TERRIFIC | GODDAMN |
| SUPER | BITCH |
| BRILLIANT | MOTHERFUCKER |
| GREAT | SHIT |
| EXCELLENT | FUCK |
| FANTASTIC | PISS |

Word search puzzle answer key is on page 174.

# Drastic Times . . .

Samantha had a miserable day shopping for bridesmaid's dresses with her sister. The good news is they found a dress. The bad news is Samantha's going to have to wear the hideous dress at her sister's wedding.

Now Samantha is out with some friends letting off some steam. The problem is Samantha's friends Dana and Simone have abandoned her for two affable med-school residents, Samantha's friend Fiona has gone home with a sinus infection, and Samantha's friend Diane went to go meet up with her boyfriend, Lonnie.

You still got us.
You can leave your hat on . . . Woo!

Samantha misses having a boyfriend to go home to. As she pulls out her wallet to pay for her drinks, a piece of paper falls out. It's the phone number of Seth Petro, a guy who she used to work with and flirt with back when she still had a boyfriend. She would never get serious with Seth; he's too much of a dog.

However . . . Samantha knows what she has to do, but she's nervous that the alcohol may be clouding her judgment.

Circle every third letter in order to spell out for Samantha what she needs to make happen now to help ease her woes.

| | | | | | | | | |
|---|---|---|---|---|---|---|---|---|
| **F** | **G** | **B** | **C** | **L** | **O** | **M** | **F** | **O** |
| **Q** | **K** | **T** | **N** | **Z** | **Y** | **X** | **M** | **C** |
| **R** | **L** | **A** | **J** | **S** | **L** | **D** | **T** | **L** |

Answer: Booty call

# Whet Thu Fack?!!

Samantha's sister has just informed Samantha that Samantha's ex is going to be invited to her wedding.

Samantha's sister met her betrothed through Samantha's ex, who has been friends with Samantha's sister's fiancé since they went to soccer camp together when they were ten.

Big Whoop! I had a swim coach who beat me when I was ten. Does that mean I have to invite him to my wedding?

Samantha's furious at the prospect of having her ex at her own sister's wedding. She's so mad that she's actually starting to lose command of the English language. While she can still speak, her pronunciation is all over the place.

Help those around Samantha make sense of her frantic ramblings before someone locks her up for good. Translate the lines below into "real" English and write them on the lines given.

1. Zis ezen't weelie habbinin, iz et? Tal mea ziz izin't habbinin.

 ____________________________________________

 ____________________________________________

2. Hou koot sea du diz tummy? Mi oon ziztur.

 ____________________________________________

 ____________________________________________

3. Du yu tink e joorie woood finet mee gilty ef eye merdurd hur fur dis?

 ____________________________________________

 ____________________________________________

4. Ov coars, eye kood cil mi hex enzdead. Ya, hi fink hi lyke zat idear mwhore. Zat's waat iyle du.

______________________________________________

______________________________________________

5. Waat's ze bezd sway tu kel zumon? I was zinken uv byink a penthur ant ledingk et luse enzide hes houz.

______________________________________________

______________________________________________

6. Du yu tink hime ufurreagtink? Da curekt anzer is, "snow!"

______________________________________________

______________________________________________

7. Waat em hi geddink zo apzet huboat? Et's snot lyke da mang hoo hi daded fur zevan-hand-huh-hav hears dumped mea ant iz nou cumink tu mi zizter's wettink. Ho, wayt, daz etzatly wuz habbinin.

______________________________________________

______________________________________________

8. Zers unlee juan wae tu rehollisticly del wit diz, hand dat's tu git druk . . . wedge iz waat hime goink tu du . . . zdardink emediedlee.

______________________________________________

______________________________________________

Answers: 1. This isn't really happening, is it? Tell me this isn't happening. 2. How could she do this to me? My own sister. 3. Do you think a jury would find me guilty if I murdered her for this? 4. Of course, I could kill my ex instead. Yeah, I think I like that idea more. That's what I'll do. 5. What's the best way to kill someone? I was thinking of buying a panther and letting it loose inside his house. 6. Do you think I'm overreacting? The correct answer is, "No!" 7. What am I getting so upset about? It's not like the man who I dated for seven-and-a-half years dumped me and is now coming to my sister's wedding. Oh, wait, that's exactly what's happening. 8. There's only one way to realistically deal with this, and that's to get drunk . . . which is what I'm going to do . . . starting immediately.

# Workin' It Out!

Samantha's started exercising again!

I gotta get back to the gym. I feel like a cow.

Without her even knowing it, something very special has started resurfacing in Samantha since she started pumping iron again. In addition to building muscle, stamina, and the ability to nod to people she knows while on a Stairmaster without looking like a complete imbecile, Samantha is building an equally important quality that she needs to be made aware of. Help Samantha discover what it is as she works off her recent meals.

Circle all of the words that have E, F, T, S, M, and L in them. Once you've done that, draw a box around the third letter in each word that you circled and then read the boxed letters from top to bottom to find out what mysterious new feeling Samantha's beginning to exercise.

| | | |
|---|---|---|
| ZUCCHINI | PORK CHOP | RUTABAGAS |
| PASTA | COFFEE | BREAD |
| CORN | CHEESE | LEEKS |
| BEETS | MUSTARD | LEMONADE |
| ROLLS | BRAN | COCOA |

Answer: Self-esteem

# hbaeasrtlteasds (heartless bastard)

Samantha's ex is now trying to win Samantha back by comparing their union to other classic pairings. But Samantha doesn't want to get back together with her ex just because he said they were like peanut butter and jelly. She can think of a number of pairings that they resemble more. Unfortunately, Samantha's thoughts are so jumbled by her ex's persistence that she's having trouble verbalizing any of them.

Below are eight pairs of words that don't go together, scrambled into each other. For example: perenacsierlss (pencils and erasers).

Help Samantha separate the words from each other so that she can use them as her own examples to her ex.

fiircee

faisihr

braadtiohss

vevgeanasl

crsotacnheds

mfiumnensy

nwueneds

hshearripnesg

Answers: 1. fire/ice; 2. fish/air; 3. baths/radios; 4. vegans/veal; 5. crotches/sand; 6.mimes/funny; 7. nuns/weed; 8. herpes/sharing

# Big, Less Big, and Put Down the Crack Pipe

Samantha is having a bit of trouble keeping everything in her life in perspective.

I'm sorry, they were all out of 2% milk. I hope 1% is okay?
Oh, so now you're out to get me too, is that it?!!!

Help Samantha gain perspective and stop sweating the small stuff by helping her recognize which issues are big, which issues are less big, and which issues she needs to put the crack pipe down for and stop wasting another moment of energy on. Place a "**B**" for Big, "**L**" for Less Big, or a "**C**" for Put Down the Crack Pipe in front of each statement.

------- 1. Samantha's younger sister is getting married and Samantha's ex is invited to the wedding.

------- 2. Samantha's cell-phone provider is trying to charge her $375 for minutes she didn't use.

------- 3. *Grey's Anatomy* is a repeat this week.

------- 4. Samantha has an important deadline for work that she's trying to meet.

------- 5. Samantha broke a dish.

------- 6. A friend of Samantha's told Samantha that a couple weeks earlier she saw Samantha's ex out on a date with Belinda Kenner, one of Samantha's least favorite people.

------- 7. Samantha's mom wants her to make a trip to her favorite yarn store, which is way out of the way for Samantha, in order to purchase her mom's favorite yarn so that she can begin to knit baby clothes for her sister's as-of-yet conceived children.

------- 8. Samantha's local market ran out of Ben & Jerry's Chocolate Chip Cookie Dough ice cream, her favorite flavor.

------- 9. Samantha's uncle had a heart attack.

------- 10. Samantha's car has a broken taillight.

------- 11. Samantha's toilet is stopped up.

------- 12. Samantha got food poisoning from a roast beef sandwich.

Answer: 1. B; 2. B; 3. B; 4. B; 5. C; 6. B; 7. B; 8. B; 9. B; 10. L; 11. L; 12. B

# what 2 Do

Samantha is having another one of those days where it feels like having anybody would be better than having no one at all. Her ex is trying to capitalize on that fact and get back into her good graces.

Samantha is of two minds at the moment. As frustrated as her ex makes her, they have a long history together that is hard for her to overlook. Help Samantha sort out her thoughts by making sense of the sentences that follow. Each sentence has double the amount of letters, mirroring the two different sides of Samantha's feelings.

1. HHee ssaayyss hhee ssttiiill lloovveess mmee..

   ______________________________________________

   ______________________________________________

2. II tthhiinnkk II mmiigghhtt ssttiiill lloovvee hhiimm..

   ______________________________________________

   ______________________________________________

3. HHee''ss ccuuttee..

   ______________________________________________

   ______________________________________________

4. HHee''ss nnoott aass ccuuttee aass hhee tthhiinnkkss hhee iiss..

   ______________________________________________

   ______________________________________________

5. WWee''vvee bbeeeenn ttooggeetthheerr ffoorr ssoo lloonngg;; wwee kknnooww eeaacchh ootthheerr ssoo wweellll.. IIttt wwoouulldd bbee nniiccee nnoott ttoo hhaavvee ttoo ssttaarrtt aallll oovveerr wwiitthh ssoommeeoonnee nneeww..

6. HHee ccaann bbee rreeaallllyy sswweeeett..

7. HHee ccaann aallssoo bbee aann iimmmmaattuurree,, sseellff--iimmppoorrttaanntt ppeecckkeerr..

8. II''mm oovveerr tthhee wwhhoollee ddaattiinngg tthhiinngg..

9. WWee hhaavvee aa lloott ooff pprroobblleemmss.. TThhaatt''ss aann uunnddeerrssttaatteemmeenntt..

10. HHee''ss nnoott aa bbaadd ccooookk..

11. IIttʼʼss ssaadd ttoo ssaayy,, bbuutt IIʼʼvvee hhaadd wwoorrssee bbooyyffrriieennddss..

12. II jjuusstt ssppeenntt tthhee llaasstt sseevveerraall mmoonntthhss ccuurrssiinngg hhiiss nnaammee..

13. IInn mmyy hheeaarrtt ooff hheeaarrttss,, II wwaanntt ttoo bbeelliieevvee tthhaatt tthheerreeʼʼss aa gguuyy oouutt tthheerree wwhhoo kknnoowwss hhooww ttoo ttrreeaatt mmee rriigghhtt,, tthhee wwaayy II ddeesseerrvvee ttoo bbee ttrreeaatteedd..

14. II lloovvee hhiimm mmuucchh iinn tthhee ssaammee wwaayy aa ssmmookkeerr lloovveess nniiccoottiinnee——II wwaanntt iitt eevveenn tthhoouugghh II kknnooww iitt mmiigghhtt kkiillll mmee..

________________________________________

________________________________________

________________________________________

15. TThhiiss iiss rriiddiiccuulloouuss!! II ccaann''tt bbeelliieevvee II''mm eevveenn ccoonnssiiddeerriinngg tthhiiss..

________________________________________

________________________________________

16. Nnoo,, nnoo,, nnoo,, nnoo,, nnoo,, nnoo,, nnoo,, nnoo,, nnoo,, nnoo,, nnoo..

________________________________________

________________________________________

Answer: 1. He says he still loves me. 2. I think I might still love him. 3. He's cute. 4. He's not as cute as he thinks he is. 5. We've been together for so long; we know each other so well. It would be nice not to have to start all over with someone new. 6. He can be really sweet. 7. He can also be an immature, self-important pecker. 8. I'm over the whole dating thing. 9. We have a lot of problems. That's an understatement. 10. He's not a bad cook. 11. It's sad to say, but I've had worse boyfriends. 12. I just spent the last several months cursing his name. 13. In my heart of hearts, I want to believe that there's a guy out there who knows how to treat me right, the way I deserve to be treated. 14. I love him much in the same way a smoker loves nicotine—I want it even though I know it might kill me. 15. This is ridiculous! I can't believe I'm even considering this. 16. No, no, no, no, no, no, no, no, no, no, no.

# Going Up?: Volume 4

Samantha's ready to ride the final uplift elevator!

This time, Samantha gets to ride in the "Re" Elevator!

The Re Elevator only has one floor to avoid.

Take a look at all of the buttons in the Re Elevator and color in all of the buttons except for the one that Samantha shouldn't hit.

## Re-

| | | | | |
|---|---|---|---|---|
| fined | flective | laxed | newed | markable |
| stored | spectable | levant | incarnated | ady |
| assured | splendent | focused | habilitated | ally pissed |
| inforced | lieved | freshed | vived | achable |
| strained | developed | deemed | silient | adjusted |

Answer: Don't hit really pissed.

# Me Loves He, Me Loves He Not

The wondrous spirit of love is alive at Samantha's sister's wedding. No one is feeling the power of love more than Samantha's ex.

They say imitation is the best form of flattery. I guess we'll see. Samantha, will you marry me?
. . .

Before Samantha has had a chance to tell her ex where he can shove his love, her ex takes the floor to make a toast.

Samantha is stunned. She just heard the four words that she's been waiting to hear for nearly eight years!

There's only one logical way for Samantha to figure out her true feelings: Me Loves He, Me Loves He Not. Samantha's so befuddled that she's decided to leave her fate up to the gods. She's going to grab the flower in front of her from its vase and pull out the petals one by one to see if she loves her ex enough to marry him.

With her ex and every guest at the wedding staring at her, waiting for an answer, Samantha needs to work fast. Help Samantha by labeling each petal either a "me loves he" petal or a "me loves he not" petal. Pick a petal to start with and place an "**L**" in the petal to represent "me loves he" and an "**N**" in the next petal to represent "me loves he not." Continue that pattern until you've marked every petal. The last petal you mark is Samantha's answer. If it's a "me loves he" petal, it means Samantha should marry her ex; however, if it's a "me loves he not" petal, she should not.

# Runaway Bride(smaid)

Great Work! Thanks to you, Samantha has her answer. Now all she has to do is get the hell out of there.

As Samantha makes a run for it, help her follow her heart out to safety.

Where's she going?
Why?
She's making a run for it.
Because that's what you do when you're not going to marry a guy. You run out on him. Haven't you ever seen a romantic comedy?

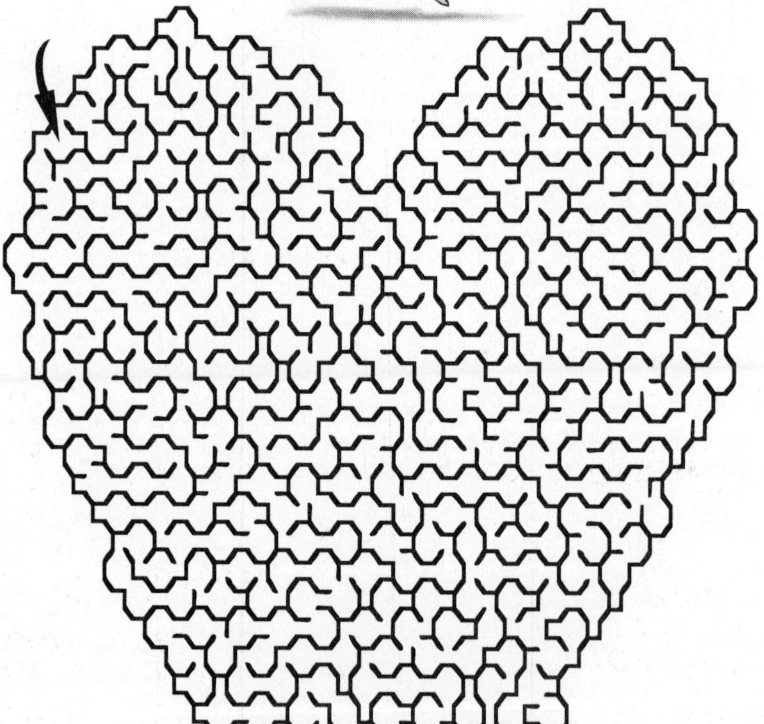

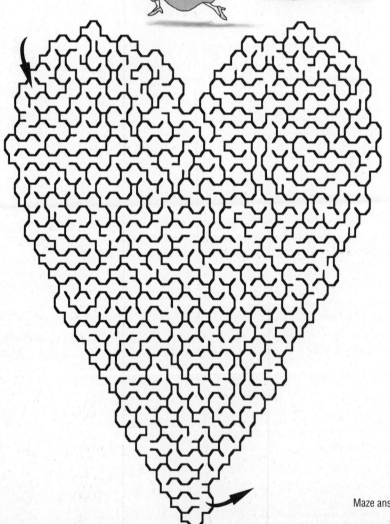

Maze answer on page 174.

# Open Heart, Tongue Tied

Samantha's almost in the clear!

She has successfully made it through the banquet hall and is about to leave her ex, her family, and dozens of her sister's and parents' friends in the dust. There's just one more obstacle . . .

*BAM!*

As if Samantha doesn't have enough to worry about . . .

Gosh, I'm sorry. I really should watch where I'm going.
Here, let me help you up.
Oh no, that's all right.

Love has a habit of hitting us at the most unexpected moments.

The last thing Samantha ever expected to happen at her sister's wedding was to fall for a caterer waiter after bashing into him because she was running away from her ex who had just proposed to her in front of everybody.

But that's no reason for Samantha not to take advantage of this moment. There's just one thing standing between Samantha and eternal bliss: Grammar.

Samantha's so dumbstruck that she's lost the ability to construct sentences correctly. Help Samantha get her words in order so she doesn't make an ass of herself and mess up this very real shot at true love.

Reorder the words in Samantha's sentences on the lines below so that she doesn't sound like Yoda.

**Samantha**

1. sorry smashed I'm that I you the into door. terrible just I feel.

______________________________________________

______________________________________________

**Sam**

It's really all right. I consider getting smashed into a door at the hands of someone as lovely as you an honor.

**Samantha**

2. sweet You so are. glad for I'm handsome to door And that smash when someone it came as time me a into was you, it someone as.

______________________________________________

______________________________________________

**Sam**

Do you think that you could give me your
phone number so that I might call you some time?

**Samantha**

3. delighted number be give I to you my would phone.

______________________________________________

______________________________________________

**Sam**

Great! You seem like a very nice person and I look forward to getting to know you better.

**Samantha**

4. Likewise. never sure someone am I glad sister's I to you expected meet my like wedding, but did I at.

______________________________________________

______________________________________________

**Sam**

Me, too. Do you like sushi? I know a great sushi restaurant.

**Samantha**

5. kidding Are me you? sushi lot I a love.

______________________________________________

______________________________________________

**Sam**

Terrific. So we can go out for sushi together.

**Samantha**

6. proposed I'm smash happy ex to, me meet which for made so safety me and into that that my door and run you.

____________________________________________________________

____________________________________________________________

**Sam**

What?

**Samantha**

7. never It's mind okay,.

____________________________________________________________

____________________________________________________________

**Sam**

All right, whatever you say.

Answer: 1. I'm sorry that I smashed the door into you. I feel just terrible. 2. You are so sweet. And I'm glad that when it came time for me to smash a door into someone, it was someone as handsome as you. 3. I would be delighted to give you my phone number. 4. Likewise. I never expected to meet someone like you at my sister's wedding, but I sure am glad I did. 5. Are you kidding me? I love sushi a lot. 6. I'm so happy that my ex proposed to me, which made me run for safety and smash into that door and meet you. 7. It's okay, never mind.

# Sam's Story

This is Sam.

Sam just got dumped.

Will you help Sam climb out of the pit of hell that is his life and stick by him as he travels down the exciting and mysterious road to recovery?!

I'll meet you on the next page. I think my ex may have called.
She didn't.
Road to Recovery


What are we waiting for?
Let's get started!

# Reeling & Dealing: Dumped Word Scramble

Sam's confused. Ever since his ex broke up with him, his emotions have been all scrambled up inside him.

Help Sam unscramble the scrambled words in his head so that he can get to those critical thoughts and feelings that have been scrambled up inside him ever since he got dumped.

Note: They start simple and become progressively more difficult . . . just like relationships.

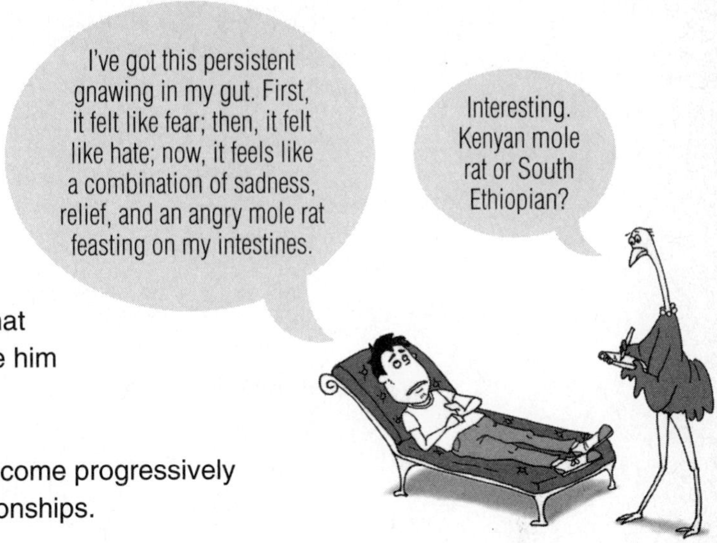
I've got this persistent gnawing in my gut. First, it felt like fear; then, it felt like hate; now, it feels like a combination of sadness, relief, and an angry mole rat feasting on my intestines.
Interesting. Kenyan mole rat or South Ethiopian?

1. TISH ____________________

2. OGDMDNA IT ____________________

3. KUFC FKCU UKCF ____________________

4. MI' OTLAYLT WRSDCEE ____________________

5. I EAHT TTAH TIBHC____________________

6. I VOEL ATHT HBCIT____________________

7. IHST CUFK SPSI KFCU STHI CFKU ISPS____________________

Answers: 1. Shit; 2. Goddamn it; 3. Fuck fuck fuck; 4. I'm totally screwed; 5. I hate that bitch; 6. I love that bitch; 7. Shit fuck piss fuck shit fuck piss

# Search Party!

Now that Sam has gotten in touch with his true feelings, he's ready to buckle down and start the real work.

Sam loved his ex very much.

I love you and I want to be with you forever.
I think I'm going to get the meatloaf.

He loved her so much that sometimes it was hard for him to recognize that they had problems.

Now the search for truth begins. Help Sam find the words and phrases hidden in the word search on the next page so that he can begin to recognize some of the important issues that contributed to his relationship's demise.

Keep in mind: It's not merely about seeking words; it's about seeking the truth.

| | | | | | | | | | | | | | | | | | |
|---|---|---|---|---|---|---|---|---|---|---|---|---|---|---|---|---|---|
| N | Y | E | N | I | H | T | I | V | H | S | H | K | E | I | T | F | V |
| O | E | P | N | Y | M | K | N | A | S | S | Y | L | Y | E | T | N | T |
| I | E | D | H | N | M | T | Y | D | L | P | I | A | E | E | F | N | B |
| T | E | D | S | E | G | P | I | A | I | I | O | N | C | A | A | T | R |
| C | E | N | I | R | L | G | H | S | R | S | A | E | S | T | I | R | E |
| N | D | E | T | P | I | D | Y | O | R | D | E | C | I | N | S | C | O |
| U | N | D | E | R | A | P | P | R | E | C | I | A | T | E | D | P | C |
| F | O | I | F | F | R | L | O | A | S | S | I | N | R | D | Y | T | N |
| S | I | H | T | T | C | O | C | K | T | E | A | S | E | N | T | L | N |
| Y | E | F | O | I | T | I | H | O | S | E | N | P | V | E | S | S | O |
| D | T | S | O | N | E | F | O | I | M | A | S | O | X | P | D | D | O |
| E | L | E | F | E | S | S | N | E | S | P | E | B | H | E | R | Y | E |
| L | U | T | P | D | E | P | D | R | S | I | L | S | F | D | D | I | P |
| I | I | E | V | G | N | I | R | A | E | B | R | E | V | O | A | T | O |
| T | N | Y | V | N | E | S | I | N | E | P | Y | S | X | C | P | E | Y |
| C | F | I | P | C | T | N | A | R | C | I | S | S | I | S | T | I | C |
| E | I | E | N | R | C | C | C | K | S | H | S | I | F | L | E | S | C |
| R | E | E | N | I | L | O | E | C | N | S | M | V | T | C | S | C | C |
| E | E | V | S | O | E | O | P | Y | E | T | L | E | I | L | F | I | E |

| | | |
|---|---|---|
| NEEDY | OEDIPAL COMPLEX | CODEPENDENT |
| SELFISH | ERECTILE | HYPOCHONDRIAC |
| OBSESSIVE | DYSFUNCTION | FRIGID |
| NARCISSISTIC | FOOT FETISH | COCKTEASE |
| LIAR | OVERBEARING | FASCIST |
| NYMPHO | UNDERAPPRECIATED | PENIS ENVY |

Word search puzzle key is on page 174.

# Return Policy

Sam and his ex were engaged to be married.

How much does that suck?

The time has come for Sam to return all the gifts that he and his ex received, and write a letter to everyone telling them that the wedding won't be happening.

The task has Sam stymied. Luckily, within the piles of presents lay just the right words Sam is looking for to alert everyone about what's happened. Can you help Sam find those words?

All you have to do is cross out all the *silverware* on the list.

Once you've crossed off the silverware, you can go ahead and cross off the *dishes*.

With the dishes out of the way, you can get rid of the *glassware*.

Finally, you can cross off the *camping equipment*. (Sam and his ex had a fantasy that if they got a bunch of camping equipment for their wedding, they'd start doing a lot of camping. There was no chance of that happening, even if they had stayed together.)

Now read the leftover words and you have Sam's letter.

dinner plates dear soup spoons friends tent and family

sugar spoon it's salt shaker over goblets she saucers

dumped me butter knives the bug repellent wedding's

soup/pasta bowls off champagne flutes i'm teapot sending

back wine glasses all the salad forks crap you teacup sent

serving spoon us grill except platter for vegetable bowl

the martini shaker creamer salad plates i'm teaspoons

going sauce boat to dinner forks need steak knives that

Answer: Dear friends and family, It's over. She dumped me. The wedding's off. I'm sending back all the crap you sent us except for the martini shaker. I'm going to need that.

# Choose your words!

Yesterday, Sam's aunt asked him if he thought he and his ex would ever get back together. Sam's response was . . .

We'll get back together when you and Uncle Jake get back together!
HAPPY BIRTHDAY AUNT

Sam's uncle died nine years ago.

Help Sam learn to control his anger and choose his words more carefully. Circle the appropriate responses to the statements on the facing page.

"You're better off":

A. Yeah, who needs love and companionship? I'm much happier being a troll.
B. You're better off getting your ass kicked.
C. I know. It's just hard right now. But everything happens for a reason, and I know that, in the end, it'll just make me stronger.
D. Fuck you.

"I really liked her":

A. Well, she's available.
B. I really liked kicking your ass two seconds from now.
C. Yeah, so did I, but it just wasn't working out. I guess that's just the way it goes sometimes.
D. Guess what? Fuck you.

"The hottest love has the coldest end."

A. That sure is a pick-me-up.
B. The smartest ass gets my cold, hard foot up it.
C. I never knew you were a student of the Greeks.
D. Fuck you and fuck you.

Answer: While the "C" responses are the most civilized and appropriate responses to all of the statements, Sam might go insane being that polite and earnest all the time. For that reason, he has the "A" responses to fall back on—not completely mean spirited, but just sarcastic enough to satisfy the demons that lurk within him. Depending on the circumstances, he might even be able to throw a "B" or a "D" response in there every once in a while, just to let off a little steam. "B" and "D" responses, however, should be reserved for special occasions only, and should never be used on anyone that could beat Sam up. The important thing for Sam to do is to assess each situation as it presents itself and then decide how much he can get away with.

# The one

One of the reasons Sam is so devastated by this breakup is because he was convinced that for once he had met "The One."

Truth be told, Sam's met "The One" more than a couple times. His first "The One" was his next-door neighbor growing up. It was doomed from the start though. He was five and convinced he was going to spend his life with her. She was forty-five and already married. After that came an endless string of other "The Ones" including: "The One" on his soccer team, "The One" he met at his cousin's bar mitzvah, "The One" who was his first kiss, "The One" who got him drunk, "The One" who introduced him to oral sex, "The One" from his global initiatives class, "The One" with the piercings, "The One" who cared for the elderly, "The One" from Zaire, "The One" who loved puppies, "The One" whose dad hated him, "The One" who was deaf, "The One" who became a nun, "The One" he gave a kidney to, and "The One" who went on to marry Sting's nephew.

Help Sam realize that the idea of The One isn't helping him, and has been getting in his way. See how many times you can find "The One" written out in the word search below.

| | | | | | | | | | | | | |
|---|---|---|---|---|---|---|---|---|---|---|---|---|
| O | O | H | T | E | E | O | N | E | O | H | E | E |
| O | E | E | T | T | N | H | T | O | N | E | N | E |
| T | O | H | T | E | T | H | T | H | E | O | H | E |
| E | O | H | E | H | E | N | T | H | E | H | N | E |
| O | N | E | H | T | N | H | T | H | E | O | N | E |
| T | E | E | N | O | E | H | T | H | E | O | N | E |
| N | N | E | N | O | E | H | T | H | E | O | N | E |
| T | E | E | N | O | E | H | T | H | E | O | N | E |
| E | E | E | N | O | E | H | T | H | E | O | N | E |
| H | O | E | N | O | E | H | T | H | E | O | N | E |
| E | E | E | O | O | E | H | T | H | E | O | N | E |
| H | E | N | N | T | E | N | T | H | E | O | N | E |
| E | E | E | N | O | E | H | T | H | N | T | N | E |
| E | O | E | T | H | T | T | T | E | T | E | H | E |

Answer: 36

# See-ya-Later-Gram

A big part of Sam's overall frustration has to do with how the relationship officially ended. Sam's ex took dumping to a whole other level. Afraid to do it herself and unable to convince any of her friends to do it for her, she went ahead and did it with a singing telegram!

I guess she thought an e-mail would be too impersonal.

Now every time Sam tells anyone about the singing telegram, the next words out of their mouth are, "So, how did the song go?" For some reason, it didn't occur to Sam to memorize the song's lyrics, as the woman was telling him that his ex had had enough.

Now Sam must summon his powers of recall so that he can satisfy the morbid curiosity of his friends and family. He's managed to dredge up most of the song's words. All that's left are the words at the end of the phrases. Sam remembers all those words, he just can't remember which words go where.

Take a look at the phrases and at the words and fill in each blank with the proper word.

You may think she's a ____________

You may say she's a ____________

But she can't find the ____________

That she knows she must ____________

So she's hired a ____________

And that singer is ____________

To sing with a ____________

That she needs to be ____________

| |
|---|
| Words |
| Smile |
| Speak |
| Singer |
| Free |
| Coward |
| Creep |
| Me |

Answer: You may think she's a coward/You may say she's a creep. But she can't find the words/That she knows she must speak. So she's hired a singer/And that singer is me/To sing with a smile/That she needs to be free.

# The Ex Factor

Sam is afraid he'll never be able to escape from the ominous presence of his ex.

But what would the world be without exes?

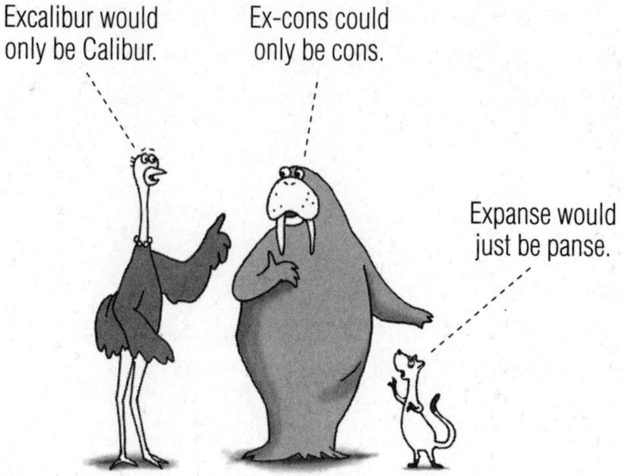
Excalibur would
only be Calibur.
Ex-cons could
only be cons.
Expanse would
just be panse.

Help Sam recognize the great importance that exes play in the world and even in his own life. Read the dialogue that follows. Fill in the blanks for the "ex" words and expose Sam to the extraordinary powers of ex.

1. The ferret says, "I gained a million pounds the last time I got dumped!"

   This means that the ferret is ex__ __ __ __ __ __ __ __ __ __.

2. The walrus says, "My ex always wanted me to be like, 'All hail the great one for she is so great! Blah, blah, blah. Hail!'"

   The walrus' ex wanted the walrus to be ex__ __ __ __ __ __.

3. The Ostrich says, “I cast you out, phantom fiancé, from this man’s spirit. Demons depart! Be gone and stay far from this creature, SUCKA!”

   The ostrich is performing an ex__ __ __ __ __ __.

4. The ferret says, “By the power vested in me, I hereby declare that you, Sam, are not responsible for the super fucked-up shit that has happened to you.”

   The ferret has ex__ __ __ __ __ __ __ __ Sam.

5. The walrus says, “Check out my genitalia!”

   The walrus is an ex__ __ __ __ __ __ __ __ __ __ __.

6. The Ostrich says, “Oftentimes, these emotionally traumatic events end up causing corresponding physical ailments. Take your clothes off and sit on this incredibly uncomfortable paper; I’ll get my listen-to-your-heart-thingamajig and poke and prod you as I attempt to make awkward small talk with you.”

   The ferret is going to give Sam an ex__ __ __ __ __ __ __ __ __.

7. The ferret says, “I’m not threatening you with this baseball bat; I’m offering you ‘protection’ for a nominal fee. It can be very dangerous out there for a single person. I would hate to see anything happen to you.”

   The ferret is attempting to ex__ __ __ __ money from Sam.

8. The ostrich says, “Hey there, Barmaid, this is Sam. He just got dumped, so you should be really nice to him and give both of us lots of free drinks.”

   The ostrich is trying to ex__ __ __ __ __ Sam’s misfortune.

Answers: 1. exaggerating; 2. exultant; 3. exorcism; 4. exonerated; 5. exhibitionist; 6. examination; 7. extort; 8. exploit

# Is It Over for Good?

Unquestionably, the most popular postbreakup question, "Is it over for good?" is the question we all hate to hear but can't help asking ourselves as well as others.

"Is it over for good?" is a wily virus that finds its way into our systems despite any and all of the elaborate barricades we've put in its way. No matter what its origin, it must be eliminated at all costs. It's the deadliest of all postbreakup questions, and if not dismissed immediately, will not only undo all the valuable work one has already done, but can also serve to prolong the recovery process by weeks, months, or even years.

Fortunately, that all ends now, thanks to the "Is It Over for Good?" Multiple-Choice Quiz. This is a quiz that you can take about your own breakups and can also administer to others. Circle the correct answer.

1. The last time I spoke to my ex, he/she . . .

    A. Asked me to take them back.
    B. Asked me to stop contacting them.
    C. Asked me for a kidney.
    D. Asked me to drop dead.

2. My ex still . . .

    A. Is in love with me.
    B. Returns my gifts.
    C. Won't give me my cat back.
    D. Denies ever knowing me.

3. My ex has changed his/her. . .

    A. Mind and wants me back.
    B. Phone number.
    C. Name to Sun Rainwater.
    D. Gender.

4. My ex's best friend . . .

A. Told me my ex misses me.
B. Told me to give up hope.
C. Tried to stab me.
D. Is now dating my ex.

5. All my friends tell me . . .

A. I still have a chance.
B. I'll get over it.
C. I'm fucked.
D. They had to choose between me and my ex, and they chose my ex.

6. When I see my ex, I think . . .

A. They're still crazy about me.
B. Where did I go wrong?
C. Who is that person they're kissing?
D. I'm in violation of my restraining order.

7. I've told my ex how I feel and they said . . .

A. That's good, because they feel the same way.
B. They wished they felt the same way, but they don't.
C. They couldn't hear me over the loud music and sexmaking.
D. They don't care; they're still going to marry my cousin.

Answer: If you answered anything other than "A" for all of them, it's over for good. If you answered "A" for all of them, it's still over for good.

# Garbage Day: Take 1

It's garbage day!

What? Can I help it if my diet consists of 3,000 to 6,000 clams per feeding?
What the hell?

Sam's garbage men have very strict rules about what you can and can't throw out and when.

Today is "Dis Day." The garbage people only want garbage beginning with "dis."

That's no problem for Sam. He's got plenty of things that start with "dis" to throw out. But there's one "dis" that Sam needs to hang on to. Can you help Sam go through his garbage and circle the one "dis" he should keep?

heveled
graced
agreeable
oriented
tant
trustful
honest
tasteful
affected
torted
tressed
appointed
advantaged
continued
infected
mayed
pirited
passionate
posable
astrous
tracted
eased
qualified
tinguished
dainful
turbed
enchanted


Answer: distinguished

# Over Lap

Sam's been reflecting.

Penny for your thoughts?
Oh . . . y'know . . . just thinking about love . . . life . . . pain . . . and sorrow.
Hmm . . . I was wondering what my damn wings are for.

The one stumbling block Sam has is that his thoughts keeping bumping into each other. Help Sam clear things up by breaking his words down for him as he takes a jog around the running track below.

The first word has been filled in for you. The rest of the words all start using part of the previous word and flow into the next one. Write the words in the blanks on the facing page.

EXAMPLE:
Clue 1: Man's best friend D O G.
Clue 2: Evil giant monster O G R E.
Clue 3: What you do with a book R E A D.

Answer: D O G R E A D.

1. What Sam is. screwed ______________
2. Something that had to be cancelled because of the breakup. ______________
3. What existed in Sam and his ex's communication. ______________
4. The opposite of together. ______________
5. Medical condition affecting the joints that Sam was in danger of getting till he finally got off his ass and took this jog around the track. ______________
6. Something Sam and his ex had too many of. ______________
7. The secretive method by which Sam may go about gathering information about his ex. ______________
8. Sam was not on his ex's one of these. ______________
9. Sam says this when he wants to say "Fuck" or "Shit" but it's inappropriate under the circumstances. ______________
10. Sam calls himself this when he wants to call himself an "Asshole" but it's inappropriate under the circumstances. ______________
11. Sam would smoke this if he could get his hands on it. ______________
12. The amount of times Sam's ex has told him it's over. ______________
13. What Sam's ex broke off. ______________
14. The part of Sam that is teetering on the edge. ______________
15. The person who might be able to help Sam with 14. ______________

Answers: 1. screwed; 2. wedding; 3. gap; 4. apart; 5. arthritis; 6. issues; 7. espionage; 8. agenda; 9. darn; 10. nincompoop; 11. opium; 12. umpteen; 13. engagement; 14. mental health; 15. therapist

# Excess Baggage!

Sam is going away for the weekend with his friends!

Don't forget to pick up some sunscreen.
And some bug repellent.
And some hash.

Sam's friends have only one rule:
Only bring what is absolutely necessary.
In other words:

# No Excess Baggage!

Help Sam take a look at what he's carrying with him and see if you can't help him shed a few pounds of it.

In addition to several items that Sam can and should do without, everything Sam's taking with him is additionally weighed down by an extra letter hiding several times within it.

Cross out the extra letter from each word in order to decipher what Sam should bring with him and what he should leave behind. When you're done, read all of the extra letters from all of the words to discover one final thing that should not make the trip with Sam.

Hint: There are four things that Sam should leave behind.

1. B S O B C K B S — **bring / leave behind**

2. F U L A U S U H L U I U G U H U T — **bring / leave behind**

3. L S L W I L M L S L U L I T — **bring / leave behind**

4. F L R L U L S T R L A L T I L O N L — **bring / leave behind**

5. S L S O S N S G S I N G S — **bring / leave behind**

6. B H I T H T H E H R H N E H S H S — **bring / leave behind**

7. I R I E I S E I N T I M I E I N T — **bring / leave behind**

8. T U N T D E R T W T E T A R T — **bring / leave behind**

Answers: 1. Bring; 2. Bring; 3. Bring; 4. Leave Behind; 5. Leave Behind; 6. Leave Behind; 7. Leave Behind; 8. Bring
Extra letters spell out bullshit.

# Digging for Buried Pleasure

Sam's so distraught by his breakup that he can't seem to find joy in anything these days.

Did ya hear? All the nations of the world got together and declared an end to war for all time!
Fuck them.
Peace Forever.

There has to be something in the world that Sam can get a little joy from. Can you help Sam and his mates dig up something that will give Sam some pleasure?

Follow the instructions on the facing page to unearth some items below that will make Sam smile.

| | | | | | | |
|---|---|---|---|---|---|---|
| C | D | B | M | G | H | O |
| Q | R | C | M | O | V | L |
| A | X | J | U | L | T | F |
| W | E | G | A | H | N | P |
| Y | D | T | B | O | K | O |
| Z | M | S | A | C | E | I |

Dig up the letter above L and below G and put it in the fifth space of Treasure Chest 1.

Dig up the two letters above A and C and put them in order in the first two spaces of Treasure Chest 3.

Dig up the three letters between W, G, H, and P and put them in order in the last space of Treasure Chest 1 and the first two spaces of Treasure Chest 2.

Dig up the two uppermost right letters and put them in the second and third spaces of Treasure Chest 1.

Dig up the uppermost left letter, the letter two lines directly below it, and the letter three lines directly below that, and put them in the first space of Treasure Chest 1, the third-to-last space of Treasure Chest 1, and the second-to-last space of Treasure Chest 3, respectively.

Who are we kidding? We could spend all night digging around for these damn letters, but Sam needs help NOW! Find a C, an L, a T, a D, an O, and an E and fill in the open spaces in that order.

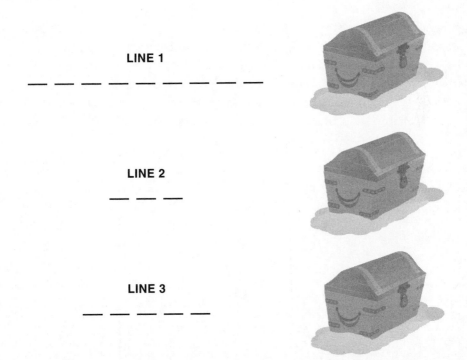

**LINE 1**

___ ___ ___ ___ ___ ___ ___ ___ ___

**LINE 2**

___ ___ ___

**LINE 3**

___ ___ ___ ___ ___

Answer: chocolate and booze

# Spin Doctor

A large part of Sam is still dizzy from the breakup.

Much of the credit for that comes from Sam's ex's mastery of the "spin." Her ability to take Sam's words, twist them around, and spit them back at Sam in a confusing and self-serving way is worthy of any of our greatest Washington spin-meisters.

Sam's ex is such a verbal alchemist that Sam often had trouble figuring out exactly what she was doing with his words.

Help Sam shed some light on his ex's mystifying mastery of the ins and outs of the English language. For every sentence Sam says, Sam's ex has a response that includes an anagram of one or more of his words. You've been given the words Sam's ex is spinning; it's your job to figure out and circle what words she's turned them into.

1. Sam: I won't accept that **it's over.**

   Ex: You have no vote, sir.

2. Sam: I've never felt so **miserable**.

   Ex: Relax. Take it easy. Go get yourself a beer, Slim.

3. Sam: Can't you see the **heartbreak** you're causing me?

   Ex: I'd much prefer to bake rather than talk about this anymore. Do you have any vanilla extract?

4. Sam: I **implore** you. Don't do this!

   Ex: Don't give me any more lip.

5. Sam: Is there **nothing** I can say to make you change your mind?

   Ex: My butt feels weird. I think I put my thong on backwards.

6. Sam: This is **bullshit**.

   Ex: I'm having dinner at Stub Hill tonight. I love that place.

7. Sam: What you're doing is completely **outrageous**.

   Ex: Letting a goat use our bathtub would be outrageous. Breaking up is just something people do.

8. Sam: How can you say our relationship isn't meeting your **expectations**?

   Ex: I thought you had the exact penis to satisfy me. I was wrong.

Answer: 1. Sam: I won't accept that **it's over**. Ex: You have no **vote sir.** 2. Sam: I've never felt so **miserable**. Ex: Relax. Take it easy. Go get yourself **a beer, Slim**. 3. Sam: Can't you see the **heartbreak** you're causing me? Ex: I'd much prefer to **bake rather** than talk about this anymore. Do you have any vanilla extract? 4. Sam: I **implore** you. Don't do this! Ex: Don't give me any **more lip**. 5. Sam: Is there **nothing** I can say to make you change your mind? Ex: My butt feels weird. I think I put my **thong in** backwards. 6. Sam: This is **bullshit**. Ex: I'm having dinner at **Stub Hill** tonight. I love that place. 7. Sam: What you're doing is completely **outrageous**. Ex: Letting a **goat use our** bathtub would be outrageous. Breaking up is just something people do. 8. Sam: How can you say our relationship isn't meeting your **expectations?** Ex: I thought you had the **exact penis to** satisfy me. I was wrong.

# Hang Up, Man!

**Two-person game! Play it with a dumped friend!**

Sam's got a little problem. He can't seem to stop calling his ex. Even worse, he has a tendency to hang up the moment she answers the phone.

See if you can get the message below to Sam before the Hang-Up Man/Woman can get to him. Find a friend to play with, preferably an obsessive, recently dumped person whose state of mind is bordering on psychotic. One of you gets to be the Guesser and the other gets to be the Hang-Up Man/Woman. The person who's guessing must be sure not to peek at the next page.

It's the guesser's job to guess letters that they think are in the words below. If they are correct, the Hang-Up Man/Woman writes the letters in all the appropriate blanks. If they are incorrect, the Hang-Up Man/Woman gets to draw a body part on the phone cord noose below. If the guesser guesses all of the right letters, the caller is saved. If all the body parts are drawn, the phone gets hung up, and the Hang-Up Man/Woman wins.

Be sure to keep a list of all the guessed letters to avoid repeats!

_ _ _ _

_ _ _ _ _ _ _

_ _ _

_ _ _

_ _ _ _ _ _ _

_ _ _ _ _ _

1 2 3
4 5 6
7 8 9
* 0 #

# Time for everyone's favorite gloomy game show—Wheel of Misfortune

Hey everybody, and welcome to Wheel of Misfortune—the show where Sam learns valuable lessons about his shitty life through the fine art of guessing letters. I'm your host, Nat Daypack, and behind me, as always, is the lovely and talented Canna Rice. Now, let's spin that wheel!

The consonants for each word have been provided for you. All you have to do is figure out which vowels go where.

The clue is: a famous martyr. The message is: perspective.

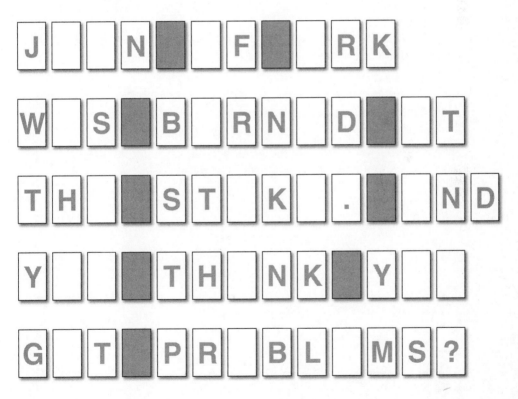

| | | | | | | | | | | | | | |
|---|---|---|---|---|---|---|---|---|---|---|---|---|---|
| J | | | N | ■ | | F | ■ | | R | K | | | |
| W | | S | ■ | B | | R | N | | D | ■ | | T | |
| T | H | | ■ | S | T | | K | | . | ■ | | N | D |
| Y | | | ■ | T | H | | N | K | ■ | Y | | | |
| G | | T | ■ | P | R | | B | L | | M | S | ? | |

Answer to Hang Up, Man!: Stop calling her. It's getting creepy.

Answer: Joan of Ark was burned at the stake. And you think you got problems?

# Star-Crossed Lovers

With all the sickening happiness in the world, Sam's been searching high and low for some comforting evidence of shared pain and misery.

The search is over! All Sam needs to do is to check out the tabloids to find a staggering supply of stirring support.

Believe it or not, even famous people face heartbreak. Help Sam take solace in the fact that he's in great company with a host of Emmy, Grammy, and Oscar winners and even downright royalty! And hey, who wouldn't want to have something in common with Roseanne?

Draw a line from the stars on the left side of the page to their former star partners on the other side of the page.

Madonna
Winona Ryder
Lyle Lovett
Brad Pitt
Donald Trump
Prince Charles
Michael Jackson
Bruce Willis
Billy Joel
Nicole Kidman
Britney Spears
David Lee Roth
Roseanne
Farrah Fawcett
Whoopi Goldberg
Mariah Carey
Mia Farrow
Sammy Hagar
Cher
Elvis Presley
Dean Martin
Ryan Phillippe
Paul Simon
Carly Simon

Sonny Bono
Lisa Marie Presley
Tom Arnold
Ted Danson
Jerry Lewis
James Taylor
Reese Witherspoon
Gwyneth Paltrow
Woody Allen
Art Garfunkel
Jennifer Aniston
Diana
Johnny Depp
Priscilla Presley
Sean Penn
Tom Cruise
Ivana Trump
Kevin Federline
Christie Brinkley
Ryan O'Neal
Van Halen
That Sony guy
Julia Roberts
Demi Moore

Answers: Madonna/Sean Penn, Winona Ryder/Johnny Depp, Lyle Lovett/Julia Roberts, Brad Pitt/Jennifer Aniston, Brad Pitt/Gwyneth Paltrow, Donald/Ivana, Prince Charles/Diana, Michael Jackson/Lisa Marie Presley, Bruce Willis/Demi Moore, Billy Joel/Christie Brinkley, Nicole Kidman/Tom Cruise, Britney Spears/Kevin Federline, David Lee Roth/Van Halen, Roseanne/Tom Arnold, Farrah Fawcett/Ryan O'Neal, Whoopi Goldberg/Ted Danson, Mariah Carey/That Sony guy, Mia Farrow/Woody Allen, Sammy Hagar/Van Halen, Cher/Sonny Bono, Elvis Presley/Priscilla Presley, Dean Martin/Jerry Lewis, Ryan Phillippe/ Reese Witherspoon, Paul Simon/Art Garfunkel, Carly Simon/James Taylor

# I Cried to Smell Few (I Tried to Tell You)

Now that his relationship is over, Sam's friends are all claiming that they'd been telling him all along that his relationship was in trouble.

I always knew that shit was fucked. I told him at the time.
We all knew they didn't have a prayer. It was common knowledge.
Remember, I told you that I thought my relationship was messed up until I saw those two together?

Sam has no recollection of any of this. That's because none of Sam's friends had the courage to tell him straight out what they really thought at the time. They only alluded to their feelings, hoping that Sam would catch their drift while avoiding the risk of indicating themselves and really pissing him off.

On the facing page are some examples of things Sam's friends said to him to try to get the message to him that he needed to move on. Can you help Sam look over his friends' appeals and try to find out just exactly what it was they were trying to say to him "all along"?

Hint: Sam's friends had a tendency to rhyme whatever it was they wanted to say to Sam with other, less harsh words. Example: Far stew hazy = Are you crazy?

1. High won't dyke fur. ____________________

2. Me's berry, berry food. ____________________

3. Why stink clue fan screw fetter. ____________________

4. He's a ditch. ____________________

5. Shoe good rump stir. ____________________

6. Fee mole ma panned crumb see. ____________________

7. We hunched pee den moo bur got hooking. ____________________

8. Bee's waitin'. ____________________

Answers: 1. I don't like her. 2. She's very, very rude. 3. I think you can do better. 4. She's a bitch. 5. You should dump her. 6. She stole a grand from me. 7. She punched me when you were not looking. 8. She's Satan.

# Up End

Sam is haunted by questions of how he'll "end up."
He's worried that this one breakup is going to shape everything
that happens to him for the rest of his life and beyond.

It's time for Sam to divide and conquer. Help Sam discover a wonderful new world of meaning to the words "end" and "up" by separating them and linking them to other words. This will rein in Sam's unhelpful obsession while instilling in him the importance of adaptability. On top of it all, you get to do a puzzle!

Each word or phrase below includes the word "end" or "up" at its beginning. Study the drawings next to the words to figure out their meanings.

Here's an example:

End<u>ocrinologist</u>

1.  Up________________

2.  Up________________

3.  Up________________

4.  Up________________

5. 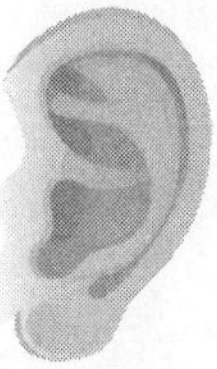 End________________

6.  Up________________

7.  Up________________

Answers: 1. Upbeat; 2. Upgrade; 3. Upright; 4. Upscale; 5. Endear; 6. Upshot; 7. Upswing

# Finger-Lickin' Blues

Sam's not enjoying his lunch.

She loved chicken fingers! Wah! We both did! It was the thing that brought us together; our mutual passion for these delectable deep-fried delicacies. Wah, wah!
It makes no sense! It makes no sense at all. Wah . . . wah, wah, wah!

Sam doesn't understand how two people could share such a passion for something and not let that passion sustain them through a lifetime.

Sam is missing the point. Will you help him get a grasp on things with the help of some spelling chicken fingers?

Every chicken finger below represents a letter. However, as you can see, some of the chicken fingers are blank. You can help by writing the correct letters on the chicken fingers that are missing letters.

**GUIDE**
Words 1 & 2: I, E, N
Words 3 & 4: O
Words 6 & 7: M, A, E

Here's a guide for which words are missing which letters: All you have to do is figure out which letters go in which blanks. NOTE: If, for example, the guide said words 4 and 5 were missing Q and Z, it would mean that both of those words had at least one Q and one Z. Some letters are used twice.

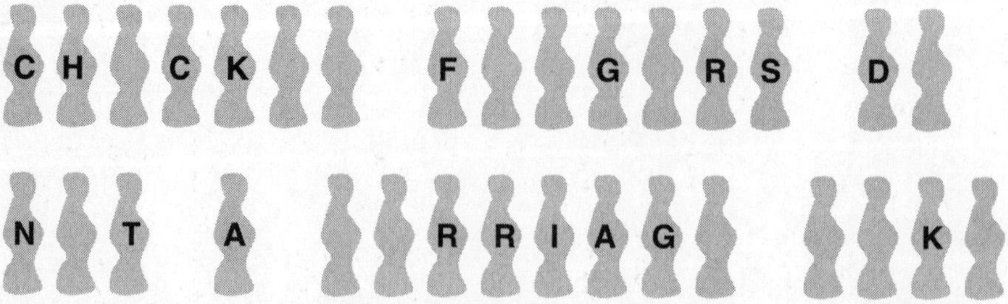
C H C K
F G R S
D
N T
A
R R I A G
K

Answer: Chicken fingers do not a marriage make.

# Selective Memory

**Two-Player Game!**

When it comes to thinking back on his relationship, Sam is in the habit of only remembering the good times . . . and not necessarily the way they really happened.

Holy Studliness Sam Man! No other man has ever made me feel this amazing!
And no other man ever will!

But there is a wealth of *other* memories that Sam's glossing over.

You know, if you didn't button your shirt so high, people would think you were less of a wiener.

These other memories, while not as arousing, are ultimately much more helpful to Sam's recovery. Help Sam revisit some of them by playing the Memory Match Game!

On the following pages are sixteen moments from Sam's relationship that Sam has chosen to forget. Each moment is written out in its own box, twice.

1. Cut out all of the boxes into cards.
2. Shuffle the cards.
3. Lay out all 32 cards on a flat surface, face down.
4. Player 1 lifts one card and then another. If the cards match, Player 1 gets to keep the cards and gets another turn. If the cards don't match, turn the cards back over and it's Player 2's turn.
5. Continue this pattern, turning the cards over and looking for matches, until every pair has been claimed. The player with the most memories wins!

The better your memory, the better you'll do!

| | | | |
|---|---|---|---|
| Ex: You know how you tell me you love me every single night before we go to bed? It's getting a little old. | Ex: Of course I'd love to get a dog, but what happens when we break up? I mean if . . . if. | Ex: Do you ever fantasize about what things would be like if we'd never met each other? | Ex: Sex is overrated. |
| Ex: I can't believe we're going to a party at Bobby Marx's house. He was my college sweetheart. I don't think I'll ever love anyone as much as I loved Bobby. | Sam: I think we'll be awesome grandparents. Ex: Let's not think about that. | Sam: I didn't know your mom was in town—I can't wait to see her! When does she leave? Ex: Yesterday. | Ex: Nathan and Dawn are so in love with each other. How do they do it? |
| Sam: I don't understand why you don't want to go on vacation together. Ex: Because that wouldn't be a vacation. | Sam: You want a massage? Ex: I'm tense enough as it is. | Sam: Did you find someone to take over your lease? Ex: No, I decided to hold on to the apartment, just because . . . um . . . you know . . . just in case . . . | Sam: I thought it would be nice to have a quiet night at home together. Ex: I'll call Caitlyn and Tabitha and see if they want to come by. |
| Ex: I'm going to the bathroom to change. Sam: Why? Ex: Because you're in here and it doesn't seem like you're leaving anytime soon. | Sam: It just occurred to me that we haven't gotten into a fight in a long time. Ex: JESUS CHRIST! IS THAT ALL YOU CAN EVER TALK ABOUT? OUR RELATIONSHIP? GIVE ME A FUCKING BREAK! | Ex: I need some space. Sam: How much space? Ex: The Eastern Seaboard. | Sam: Will you marry me? Ex: Uh . . . hmm . . . ooh . . . well . . . yikes . . . let me see . . . whoa . . . damn . . . yea . . . uh . . . eek . . . crap . . . hee . . . bu, bu, bu . . . oh . . . okay . . . what the hell . . . why not? |

| | | | |
|---|---|---|---|
| Ex: You know how you tell me you love me every single night before we go to bed? It's getting a little old. | Ex: Of course I'd love to get a dog, but what happens when we break up? I mean if . . . if. | Ex: Do you ever fantasize about what things would be like if we'd never met each other? | Ex: Sex is overrated. |
| Ex: I can't believe we're going to a party at Bobby Marx's house. He was my college sweetheart. I don't think I'll ever love anyone as much as I loved Bobby. | Sam: I think we'll be awesome grandparents. Ex: Let's not think about that. | Sam: I didn't know your mom was in town—I can't wait to see her! When does she leave? Ex: Yesterday. | Ex: Nathan and Dawn are so in love with each other. How do they do it? |
| Sam: I don't understand why you don't want to go on vacation together. Ex: Because that wouldn't be a vacation. | Sam: You want a massage? Ex: I'm tense enough as it is. | Sam: Did you find someone to take over your lease? Ex: No, I decided to hold on to the apartment, just because . . . um . . . you know . . . just in case . . . | Sam: I thought it would be nice to have a quiet night at home together. Ex: I'll call Caitlyn and Tabitha and see if they want to come by. |
| Ex: I'm going to the bathroom to change. Sam: Why? Ex: Because you're in here and it doesn't seem like you're leaving anytime soon. | Sam: It just occurred to me that we haven't gotten into a fight in a long time. Ex: JESUS CHRIST! IS THAT ALL YOU CAN EVER TALK ABOUT? OUR RELATIONSHIP? GIVE ME A FUCKING BREAK! | Ex: I need some space. Sam: How much space? Ex: The Eastern Seaboard. | Sam: Will you marry me? Ex: Uh . . . hmm . . . ooh . . . well . . . yikes . . . let me see . . . whoa . . . damn . . . yea . . . uh . . . eek . . . crap . . . hee . . . bu, bu, bu . . . oh . . . okay . . . what the hell . . . why not? |

# Card hearted

Sam's ex let Sam know that when she broke up with him it was going to be a while before she could deal with seeing or speaking to him.

Like how long?
I don't know . . . less than a millennium.

Sam's been going out of his mind trying to respect his ex's wishes and has decided that a good compromise is to send her a card. After all, she said she didn't want to see or speak to him; she didn't say anything about receiving pathetic and desperate manifestos in the form of greeting cards.

Sam needs help. Will you assist Sam in choosing the calmest and clearest words he can come up with for the card?

Circle the letters that you feel are the most apt for Sam's situation.

1. My Dearest
   A. Friend,
   B. Harpy,
   C. She-devil,
   D. Snookie,

2. Now that some time has passed since
   A. we parted ways,
   B. you canned my ass,
   C. you ripped out my heart with your bare hands,
   D. you pretended not to want to be with me anymore, which we both know is completely ludicrous,

3. I've had a lot of time to
   A. digest the magnitude of your decision.
   B. curse your unholy name.
   C. build a shrine to you out of everything I have that reminds me of you.
   D. drink.

4. So, why am I writing you, you're probably asking yourself? Well, I guess the simplest answer is because
   A. there are still some things I feel unresolved about and thought that this card would be the least obtrusive way to reach out to you while still having the satisfaction of making a little contact with you.
   B. you fucking owe me!
   C. I know that once you receive this card, you'll come running back to me.
   D. I plan to haunt you for the rest of your days.

5. I realize now that our relationship wasn't
   A. perfect.
   B. as kinky as you would've liked, but I'm prepared to remedy that.
   C. all that bad, and you're fucked if you think you're ever going to find a better deal, because let's face it, you're hardly a catch.
   D. cool enough for you. Ooh, you're so coool, I can't even stand how cooool you are. Just soooo coool.

6. So, I just wanted to check in and say
   A. hey!
   B. eat shit!
   C. I'm ready for you to take me back!
   D. If you ever want to see your kitty alive again, you better get your ass over here!

7. Obviously, things ended
   A. abruptly between us.
   B. when you dumped me.
   C. on a bad note, because you suck.
   D. because you were overwhelmed by the sheer magnitude of your passion for me.

8. I just want you to know that
   A. despite everything that's happened, I hope that we'll eventually be able to find a way to be friends. Because you really mean a lot to me and I would hate to think that on top of losing you as my girlfriend, I had also lost you as my friend. My dear friend. That would really break my heart.
   B. I can't help hating your guts.
   C. I'm leaving the front door unlocked. Come back whenever you're ready and I promise we never have to speak of this again.
   D. I won the lottery.

9. That's all I really have to say for now. I hope we can hang out some time, when you feel ready. In the meantime,
   A. are you ready to hang out yet?
   B. take care of yourself.
   C. fuck off many times.
   D. I'm redoing our bedroom. I wanted it to be a surprise, but I just can't keep it in any longer. I can't wait for you to see it, Sweetie!

10. ____________,
   A. Best,
   B. Yours,
   C. Love, love, love, love!
   D. Did I mention that you should fuck off?

—Sam

Answers*: 1. A; 2. A; 3. A; 4. A; 5. A; 6. A; 7. A; 8. A; 9. B; 10. A

*Unless you want an FBI file opened up on Sam. In which case, go crazy.

# You Say Tomato, I Say You Broke My Fucking Heart

Sam's friend Siegel just got dumped.

It must be contagious!

Sam and Siegel have been having trouble finding common ground as they compare notes. They are feeling all the same things; it's just the words they're using to describe their feelings that are different. Help Sam and Siegel commiserate by looking at both of their feelings and drawing a line between the matching ones.

| Siegel | Sam |
|---|---|
| Despair | Umbrage |
| Aggravation | Queasiness |
| Rage | Animosity |
| Resentment | Shitty |
| Nausea | Irritation |
| Fear | Fury |
| Hopelessness | Anguish |
| Bitterness | Fucked |
| Wacko | Dread |
| Apathy | Befuddled |
| Confused | Lassitude |
| Weariness | Ennui |
| Crappy | Despondency |
| Screwed | Crazier than a shithouse rat |

Answers: Despair/Anguish, Aggravation/Irritation, Rage/Fury, Resentment/Umbrage, Nausea/Queasiness, Fear/Dread, Hopelessness/Despondency, Bitterness/Animosity, Wacko/Crazier than a shithouse rat, Apathy/Ennui, Confused/Befuddled, Weariness/Lassitude, Crappy/Shitty, Screwed/Fucked

# Prior-a-Tease

I'm trying to decide if I should call my mom because it's her birthday or go stand under my ex's window and sing to her with the hope of winning back her love.
Hmm . . . that's a tough one.

Sam is suffering from what is known in polite society as a lack of perspective. Or, in impolite society, as having your head up your ass.

Help Sam gain some much-needed perspective by prioritizing some of the things he needs (and doesn't need) to do. Read the following eight sets of things Sam is considering doing. Label them in order of importance from 1 to Are You Fucking Nuts? Place a **1** in front of the top priority activity, a **2** in front of the next most important activity (or 2nd most important), and an **F** for Are You Fucking Nuts? in front of the least pressing activity.

## A.

----------- Sign up for a Save-n-Smile Super Store Savings card in order to receive discounted goods upon next visit to any and all Save-n-Smile Super Stores nationwide.

----------- Clean apartment in order to feel a greater sense of order both physically and mentally while also providing a much-needed sense of accomplishment.

----------- Make a paper mâché bust of President Grover Cleveland (ex's favorite American President) to present to ex as a President's Day gift.

## B.

---------- Visit ailing grandfather.

---------- Purchase aluminum foil.

---------- Bug ex's home in order stay up to date on her current comings and goings.

## C.

---------- Make a healthy and delicious home-cooked meal that will provide much needed nourishment absent from diet since breakup, in addition to a minor feeling of triumph.

---------- Watch reruns of *The Fresh Prince of Bel-Air*.

---------- Create a list of all wrongs perpetrated throughout the duration of the relationship, why said wrongs will never be committed again, and e-mail list to ex with hope of reconciliation.

## D.

---------- Exercise.

---------- Pay a visit to ex's parents.

---------- Search for the ever elusive, mythical Yeti.

## E.

---------- Reach out to friends.

---------- Stare at navel.

---------- Begin process of adopting a child, since all ex ever really wanted was to be a mother.

## F.

........... Leave the house for the first time in two-and-a-half weeks.

........... Carve faces out of potatoes.

........... Purchase tickets for romantic Venetian getaway with ex.

## G.

........... Volunteer at a charitable organization.

........... Play hide-and-go-seek with self.

........... Show up at ex's house with all earthly possessions and insist on moving in.

## H.

........... Sleep less than thirteen hours a day.

........... Call every one of ex's friends and relatives and tell them why she should take you back.

........... Drink as much Hawaiian Punch Red as possible.

Answers: A. 2, 1, F; B. 1, 2, F; C. 1, 2, F; D. 1, F, 2; E. 1, 2, F; F. 1, 2, F; G. 1, 2, F; H. 1, F, 2

# Garbage Day: Take 2

It's garbage day again!

Are you kidding me?
What? Can I help it if I shed most of my hair in June and July?

Today, Sam's garbage people only want garbage beginning with "over."

Can you help Sam go through his garbage and circle the three "overs" that he should keep?

rated
blown
come
drawn
joyed
heated
reacting
matched
powered
compensating
run
medicated
ruled
burdened
cast
thrown
whelmed
hauled
achieving
simplified

Answers: overjoyed, overachieving, overhauled

# The Heart of the Matter

Sam's ex has finally responded to the card that Sam sent her!

Sam is so nervous about reading the letter that the words are all dancing around on the page. It's a long, complex letter, but at the heart of it are two very important messages that Sam needs to hear.

Read all words with a heart in front them to find out what Sam's ex has to say.

=help /wink ❤dear %fritter #ringworm <detergent +pistol =gringo ❤Sam #halibut /bandit ❤Thank =juice +curtain ❤you #constable /investigation +Byzantine ❤for /odor ❤your =mellifluous %conniption ❤card %grandpa =Miami /Brenda +viceroy ❤It <decaying /freemason ❤means <tortuous #clamp ❤a +holster ❤lot =blorperg +trench ❤to /horrendous <perpendicular ❤me #graphic <gurgle /bursting ❤that #sacred ❤you +anesthetize =guilder ❤don't <crepes ❤hate /journey <hepatitis ❤me #rampage <sinusitis ❤P.S. =pony ❤I'm #judicious /boney ❤in +renegade <flock ❤love =elvis ❤with #task <shrimp ❤somebody /Per ❤else +Trench /fur

Answer: Dear Sam, Thank you for your card. It means a lot to me that you don't hate me. P.S. I'm in love with somebody else.

# The Color of Sanity

Sam's been crying so much recently that he's contracted a mild case of temporary colorblindness.

Sam's colorblindness is severe enough that he can no longer differentiate between his plethora of prescription antidepressants and allergy medication. Help Sam avoid even greater depression, and possibly a trip to the E.R. to have his stomach pumped, by adding another coat of color to his army of antidepressants.

Each pill is labeled with at least one number. Check the color index to see which colors should be used for which numbers.

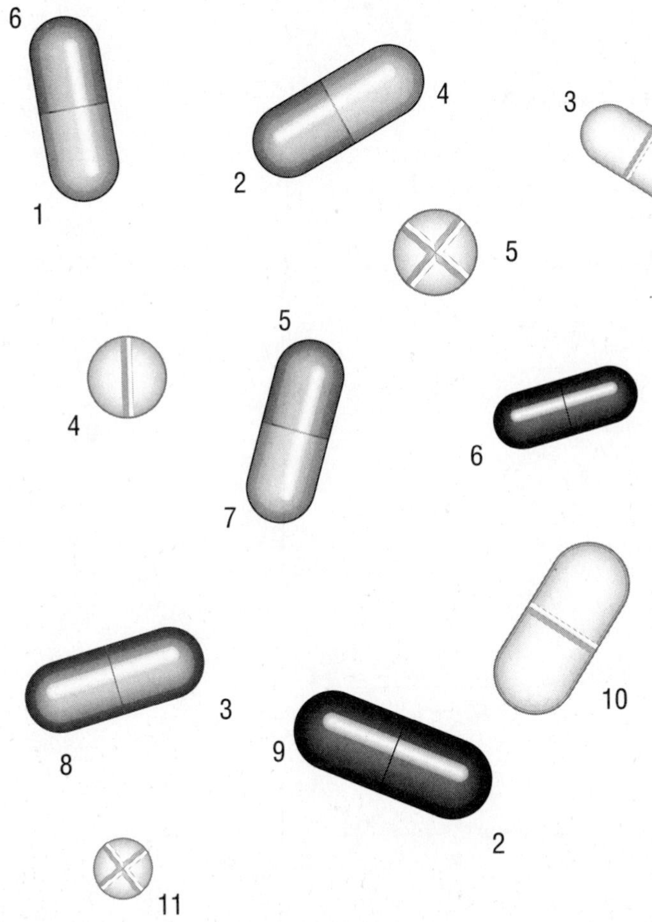
6
1
4
2
3
5
5
4
6
7
3
8
10
9
2
11

1. Green
2. Orange
3. Red
4. Blue
5. Dark Blue
6. Yellow
7. Light Yellow
8. White
9. Pink
10. Peach
11. Mauve

sam

# Really, Really Madlibs

Sam just found out that his ex is in love with someone else.

Do me a favor and don't bash any more limbs into the wall.
It's going to be hard enough to get you out as it is.

Sam's so beside himself he doesn't even know where to begin to start cursing. Help Sam channel his anger by giving him the prefect profanity to fuel his fury.

**What the** ______________________ **?! I can't believe this** ______________________ **!**
Vulgar Slang Exclamation — Vulgar Slang Noun

**After all the** ______________________ ______________________ **I put up with,**
Vulgar Slang Adjective/Adverb — Vulgar Slang Noun

**she goes and kicks me right in the** ______________________ **!**
Vulgar Slang for part of anatomy

**I feel like such a** ______________________ **!** ______________________ **!**
Vulgar Slang Noun — Foreign Slang Exclamation

**I'm totally ______________________ ______________________!**
Vulgar Slang Adjective/Adverb    Vulgar Slang Exclamation

**I'm glad this ______________________ ______________________ is over!**
Vulgar Slang Adjective/Adverb    Vulgar Slang Noun

**She can kiss my ______________________! She'll be sorry because I'm**
Vulgar Slang for part of anatomy

**gonna ______________________ rock the ______________________ out of this**
Vulgar Slang Adverb    Vulgar Slang Noun

**______________________ life! ______________________!**
Vulgar Slang Adjective/
Adverb Compound Word    Vulgar Slang Exclamation

**______________________! ______________________! ______________________!**
Vulgar Slang Exclamation    Vulgar Slang Exclamation    Vulgar Slang Exclamation

**______________________!**
Vulgar Slang Exclamation

# Upward to Thine Arse

Sam has gotten his hands on a tremendously insightful breakup self-help book written during the Renaissance by Phil Shakespeare, third cousin of Bill.

Fair maiden, thou art more lovely than the winter is wintry. I beseech thee, throw thou cares to yon wind and return to my favor to become mine wife.
No-ith.

Of all the self-help books Sam has come across, this book has resonated with him the most. There's just one drawback; much of the language of Phil Shakespeare's time is unfamiliar to Sam. Will you help Sam find the proper translations to some of the words and phrases that keep popping up regularly in Phil's book?

Place yon characters hitherto pertinent digits. (Put the letters in front of the numbers.)

A. bite me
B. bullshit
C. shit bits
D. asshole
E. son of a bitch
F. goddamn it
G. mother fucker
H. douche bag
I. blow it out your ass
J. eat shit and die

------- 1. Lord condemn the thing to hell

------- 2. matriarchal copulater

------- 3. flush sack!

------- 4. masculine offspring of a feminine tail wagger

------- 5. excrement morsels

------- 6. masticate upon my quintessence

------- 7. blast this from thy haunches

------- 8. feast upon feculence and cease to exist

------- 9. uncastrated male bovine excrement

------- 10. donkey aperture

Answers: 1. F; 2. G; 3. H; 4. E; 5. C; 6. A; 7. I; 8. J; 9. B; 10. D

# Celebrity Ex Tape

Sam's decided that since his ex won't really have anything to do with him, the only effective way to reach her and make her jealous enough to want him back is through a celebrity sex-tape scandal.

I don't know, man. I was filmed doin' the deed by the Discovery Channel and I'm still trying to live it down.

Sam has written a bunch of letters to celebrities, pleading his case and asking them for their help, but he forgot to put the names of the people he's writing to at the top of the letters. Now Sam can't remember which letter goes to whom. Can you read the letters and help Sam figure it out?

1. Dear ________________,

You are the best actress. I loved it when you tried to get inside the mind of Hannibal Lecter, and also when you were the girl who lived in the woods and babbled all the time. Will you have sex with me so that I can get back at my ex?

2. Dear ________________,

You are the coolest person on the planet. I love it how on your show everyone opens up to you and tells you about their lives. It must be super fun to be so amazingly powerful and have more money than God. Can we have sex sometime? I think it would be really fun. How about a three-way with your buddy, Dr. Phil?

3. Dear _________________,

If your lovin' is anywhere near as tasty as your baked goods, sign me up!

4. Dear _________________,

I would never want to have sex with Simon because he's too critical. And I wouldn't want to sleep with Randy because I don't like to be called dog. But I'd love to have sex with you because you're always so loving and drunk.

5. Dear _________________,

As a big-time politician, you're used to helping people, and I need a lot of help. I got dumped, and so now I'm looking for someone to have sex with me so I can get back at my ex. I know you're married, but your husband has sexual relations with other people, so why shouldn't you?

6. Dear _________________,

You are one of the classiest, most dignified, and most respected actresses of the last sixty years. That is why I would love to have sex with you if you would let me. Also, because I want to get back at my ex and that would make her very jealous. She loved you in your Emmy Award–winning role as Jessica Fletcher, and also as the voice of Mrs. Potts in *Beauty and the Beast*. Stay cool.

7. Dear _________________,

I'm trying to fulfill my DESTINY because "I'm a survivor and I'm not gonna give up." You're Bootylicious. Will you make a sex tape with me? Your videos are so hot, they practically are already.

8. Dear _________________,

My name is Sam, and I am one of your biggest fans. You were so funny when you watched Meg Ryan pretend to have an orgasm in a deli, and you are always so funny when you host the Oscars. Will you help me make a sex tape? It would be Mahvalis.

Answers: 1. Jodi Foster 2. Oprah 3. Betty Crocker 4. Paula Abdul 5. Hillary Clinton 6. Angela Lansbury 7. Beyoncé 8. Billy Crystal

# Symbolic Gesture

Sam's ex has sent him another card!

To make the situation more confusing, Sam's ex wrote this letter in code. Use the key below to help Sam decode her card.

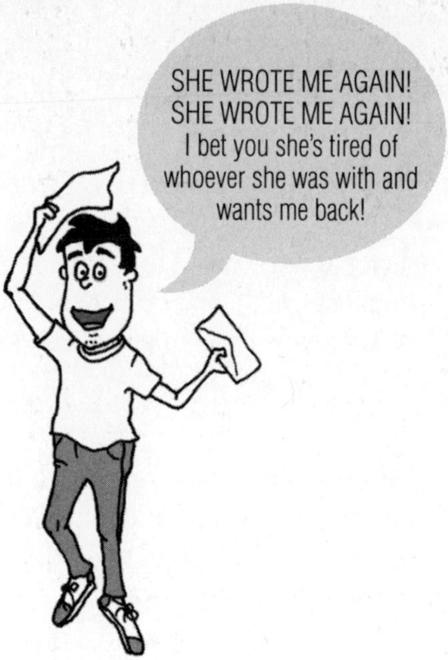
SHE WROTE ME AGAIN! SHE WROTE ME AGAIN! I bet you she's tired of whoever she was with and wants me back!

**KEY**

| | | |
|---|---|---|
| $ = A | ^ = H | # = P |
| ? = B | * = I | " = R |
| % = C | ; = L | : = S |
| / = D | ( = M | - = W |
| + = E | < = N | |
| > = F | ! = O | |

**/ + $ "    : $ (**

***    ^ ! # +    - +    % $ <    ? +    > " * + < / :**

***    $ (    $    ; + : ? * $ <**

Answer: Dear Sam/I hope we can be friends/I am a lesbian

# Letter Speak

Sam's been racking his brain for some foreshadowing of his ex's conversion to lesbianism during their relationship.

She really loved asparagus. Is that a lesbian vegetable?

As long as Sam keeps trying to find one specific piece of evidence, he's going to keep coming up short. However, if he takes the time to painstakingly analyze what his ex had to say to him during their final conversation, he'll receive positive confirmation of her leanings.

Will you help Sam? All you have to do is grab a letter from each sentence. In the case of the first sentence, you grab the first letter and put it on the first blank below. For the second sentence, you take the second letter. The third sentence, the third letter, and so on and so on, all the way up to the tenth letter of the tenth sentence.

1. I can't go on like this.
2. I'm through playing games.
3. I can't understand why you can't just let it go.
4. Will you give me a break?
5. I'm feeling very frustrated right now.
6. This is not how I expected you to react.
7. Please believe me when I tell you it's over.
8. I'm not going to keep going over this.
9. Are you deaf?
10. I'm so done. And by the way, I'm done.

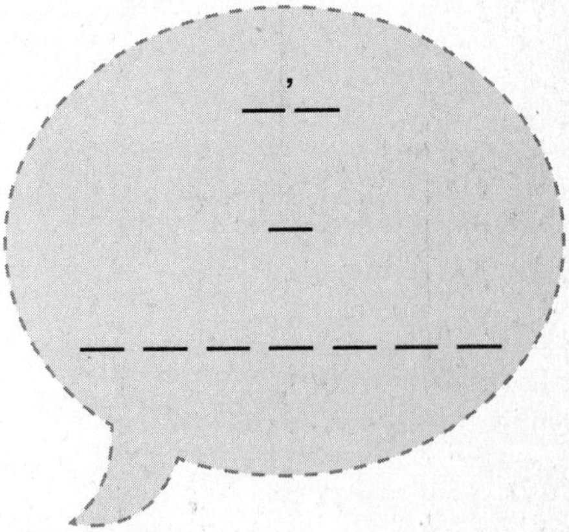

Answer: I'm a lesbian

# The Tree of Strife

The night Sam got dumped, he went out to his backyard and wept like a baby.

Unbeknownst to Sam, his tears that night reawakened the dormant earth of his backyard and watered its fertile soil. The result is a magnificent tree birthed from the pain and anger of Sam's predicament.

With the recent news that Sam's ex is in love with a woman, it seems like a perfect time for Sam to go out and look after his tree.

Unfortunately, Sam hasn't tended to the tree for a while, so it's starting to decompose. Will you help Sam nurture the parts of the tree that need attention and bring them back to life? You can do this by fertilizing the parts of the branches that have fallen off. (Fill in the empty circles with the proper letters.)

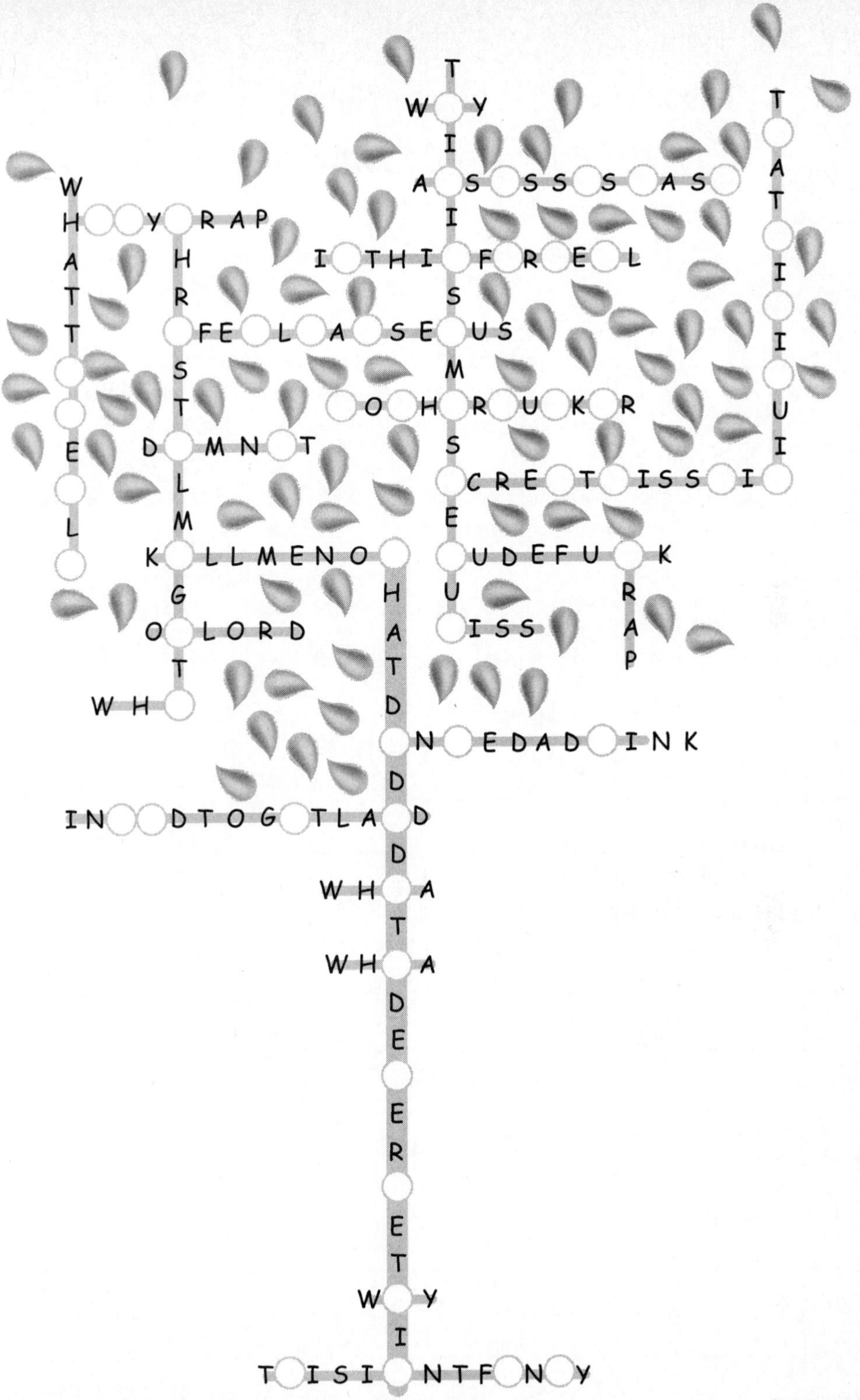

T
W Y
A S SS S AS
T
W
H Y RAP
I THI F R E L
FE L A SE US
O H R U K R
D MN T
CRE T ISS I
K LLMENO
UDEFU K
O LORD
ISS
RAP
WH
N EDAD INK
IN DTOG TLA D
WH A
WH A
W Y
T ISI NTF N Y


Answers on page 174.

# Time for another round of everyone's favorite gloomy game show— Wheel of Misfortune

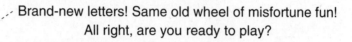

Brand-new letters! Same old wheel of misfortune fun! All right, are you ready to play?

Once again, the consonants for each word have been provided for you. All you have to do is figure out which vowels go where.

The clue is: a royal person. The message is: gratefulness.

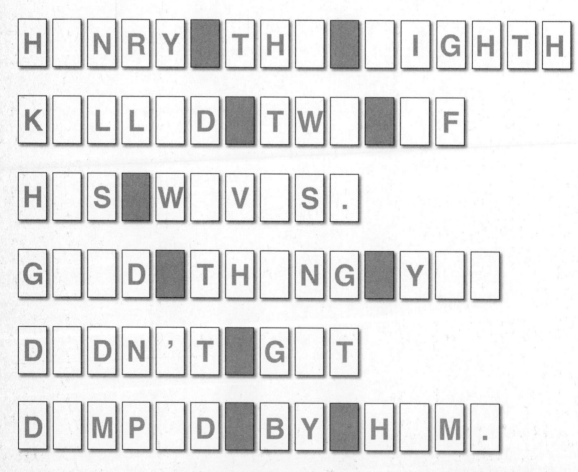

| H | _ | N | R | Y | | T | H | _ | | _ | I | G | H | T | H |
|---|---|---|---|---|---|---|---|---|---|---|---|---|---|---|---|
| K | _ | L | L | _ | D | | T | W | _ | | _ | F | | | |
| H | _ | S | | W | _ | V | _ | S | . | | | | | | |
| G | _ | _ | D | | T | H | _ | N | G | | Y | _ | _ | | |
| D | _ | D | N | ' | T | | G | _ | T | | | | | | |
| D | _ | M | P | _ | D | | B | Y | | H | _ | M | . | | |

Answer: Henry the eighth killed two of his wives. Good thing you didn't get dumped by him.

# Piec Ing It To Ge Ther

Sam's fond of saying that he didn't see it coming.

What are you doing?
I'm tearing up her belongings in a symbolic reaction to her tearing up of my heart.
That makes as much sense as smoking to lose weight.

The reason Sam didn't see it coming is because he did everything in his power not to. Now it's time for Sam to face the facts. There's evidence throughout his apartment foreshadowing his relationship's ultimate demise. Help Sam reassemble his ex's Post-its that he tore in the aftermath of the breakup. Draw a line between each half. They will provide Sam with the evidence that his ex's decision to dump him was not made in haste.

paper towels
dump
call
change
out
buy
mom
move
become
water filter
out
sam
a lesbian
work

Answers: call mom, change water filter, dump sam, work out, move out, buy paper towels, become a lesbian

# Dumped Through the Ages

Many of us, Sam included, like to believe that we're the first person ever to have been dumped. Obviously, that couldn't be further from the truth.

Help Sam recognize this fact by filling in the **Torture Timeline.**

Place the appropriate number under the year it corresponds to.

| 7000 B.C. | 2550 B.C. | 260 B.C. | 0 | A.D. 1350 |
|---|---|---|---|---|
| ---------- | ---------- | ---------- | ---------- | ---------- |

1. We had just left the malt shop and were on our way to the Sock Hop when he asked me for his pin back because he decided he'd rather go steady with Mary Sue Jenny Betty Ellen Rodgers. He got his pin back all right. I think there's still a scar.

2. My ex was a real artsy-fartsy type. Always going on about enlightenment. When Leo first showed us the Mona Lisa, I was like, "I don't get it." That was the end of that relationship.

3. We get on the boat for the New World because we're all gung-ho about escaping religious persecution and all that jive, then the second we push off he's like, "I want out." Are you kidding me? I left England for this bullshit?

4. I was building pyramids for this real dickhead of a pharaoh and datin' this sweet little chickie. She comes to me one day all teary eyed and tells me her parents don't want her dating a slave. Story of my life.

5. I figured if anyone could save my relationship it would be Jesus. But no such luck. And I got him to talk to my ex personally.

A.D. 1507 A.D. 1620 A.D. 1955 A.D. 1969 A.D. 1984

6. We were sitting around a cozy fire, which my friend Chris had just invented a couple of weeks earlier. She tells me she wants to break up with me because she's not attracted to my powerful jaw and thick eyebrow ridges. Yea, right! Like she was really going to find anyone without those features. It was like a spear going through my heart, even though they didn't exist yet.

7. I showed up at my significant other's house in parachute pants, high-top sneakers, a Live Aid T-shirt, one glove, Cindi Lauper hair, and carrying a Rubik's Cube. My significant other asked if I knew how to break dance. I said, "No." She said, "Well you're about to learn," then broke up with me.

8. So, I had the black plague. Is that really a good enough reason to break it off with a guy?

9. You would think that as a gladiator I would never get dumped. Guess again.

10. I got dumped at Woodstock, but I was trippin' so hard at the time, it was three years before I realized I was single.

Answers: 1. a.d. 1955; 2. a.d. 1507; 3. a.d. 1620; 4. 2550 b.c.; 5. 0; 6. 7000 b.c.; 7. a.d. 1984; 8. a.d. 1350; 9. 260 b.c.; 10. a.d. 1969

# Ball Bearings

Sam decided to go out and shoot some hoops to try to take his mind off the fact that his ex no longer loves him, doesn't want to have anything to do with him, loves someone else, and changed her sexual preference.

It isn't going too well.

Shoot it!
Come on, shoot it up, yo!
Shoot the ball!
00
I'm like a homosexual missionary. Traveling the globe, converting straight people to homosexuality the world over.

Sam needs a good dose of encouragement. Can you help? All you need to do is look at the letters on Sam's basketball. If you start at the top and read every other letter on the ball, and go all the way around two times, you'll get a special message to deliver to Sam.

START
S o o u w a h r a e t s i t f i y l o l u o r n e e x h i o s t g m a o y f y o

Answer: So what if your ex is gay. You are still one hot mofo.

# Stealth help

Sam has taken his dilemma to a professional: Stony Hopkins.

Stony Hopkins
Mine-&-a-Half Strides

Sam spent more money than his grandfather made in a lifetime this weekend to attend a three-day seminar sponsored by the Stony Hopkins Institute. Although Sam didn't see Stony in person for the first two-and-nine-tenths days of the seminar, Stony made an appearance for the last five minutes of the seminar, at which time Sam got to tell him his story and ask Stony if he should try to win his ex back.

Stony answered with a fascinating and archaic answer in what can only be described as "Stony Speak." Will you help Sam translate Stony's answer to English so that Sam can take in Stony's wisdom and let it guide him? All you have to do is take the first letter from each of Stony's words and place them in the blanks to discover Stony's real response to Sam's question of whether he should try to get back together with his ex or not.

**Harness own worth**

**Hail individual growth habits**

**Admit rendering errors**

**Yes offers unity**

_ _ _   _ _ _ _   _ _ _   _ _ _?

Answer: How high are you?

# Grid Locked

Sam's boss is an asshole.

Today, Sam's boss is an extra big asshole because he just found out that Sam's ex has become a lesbian. Sam's boss' response to this news . . .

She went queer on him? Ha! He's an ever bigger pansy than I thought!

Now Sam has a decision to make: how to respond.

Sam is so programmed to evade conflict with his boss that he wouldn't know what to say even if he wanted to let his boss have a piece of his mind. Which he does. Help Sam weave his way to a proper response. Below are six scrambled alphabet grids or scramphabets. Each scramphabet has one letter of the alphabet missing from it. Find the missing letter from each one and then put them all together to form Sam's response.

H Z C N D I K L M W O E Y F A G P U Q J R T V X S

N C B K M Z O A S H E Y D J X F G W I P U R Q T V

R K X Z A S H B W C Q F N U M E Y B T D J G L I P

B N D I L M Z O E Y T F X S A H Q V C G R K P U J

Z O S H T E Y N F P G Q U V K C W I X A D J L B R

K S B L W R P C X Q F N U A H J Z M O Y V T D G I

Answer: Blow me

# Do the Math

Sam's out of work!

He got fired after telling his boss to blow him after his boss called him a pansy because Sam's ex is a lesbian.

Don't feel bad.
It could've been worse.
Yea. He could've taken him up on the offer.

Sam has to do some serious number crunching to find out exactly where he is now.

Can you help Sam with this process? He has a very unique method for figuring these things out. On the facing page is a list of numbers. Each number corresponds to its place in the alphabet. Change each number into its letter counterpart to help Sam discover where he stands.

sam

You can use the AlphaNumber Index at the bottom of the page as a guide.
Write the letters of the words over the corresponding numbers.

7 5 20 20 9 14 7

4 21 13 16 5 4

+

21 14 5 13 16 12 15 25 13 5 14 20

=

20 23 9 3 5

1 19

6 21 3 11 5 4

| A | B | C | D | E | F | G | H | I | J | K | L | M | N | O | P | Q | R | S | T | U | V | W | X | Y | Z |
|---|---|---|---|---|---|---|---|---|---|---|---|---|---|---|---|---|---|---|---|---|---|---|---|---|---|
| 1 | 2 | 3 | 4 | 5 | 6 | 7 | 8 | 9 | 10 | 11 | 12 | 13 | 14 | 15 | 16 | 17 | 18 | 19 | 20 | 21 | 22 | 23 | 24 | 25 | 26 |

Answer: Getting dumped + unemployment = Twice as Fucked

# Swetchang Tiems

Sam finally caved in and went to his ex's place to speak to her. Although she won't let him in, she's agreed to speak to him from the window.

Which question should I ask first?
Not "Will you take me back if I buy you a yacht?"

In addition to the time, distance, and sexual preference that now separates Sam and his ex, there's another new factor: Language.

Sam's ex sounds different. All her vowels seem to be leaping out of her words and are being replaced by other vowels.

Help Sam get to the root of what she's saying by finding the right vowels for each word.

**Sam: Can we get together, just to talk?**
**Ex: Thari's ne paunt. E'm e lisbaen naw.**

1. __________ __________ __________. __________ __________ __________ __________.

**Sam: I know. When did you become a lesbian?**
**Ex: U've olweys bin e lisbaen.**

2. ________ ________ ________ ________ ________.

**Sam: If you've always been a lesbian, then why did you go out with me?**
**Ex: E dadn't knuw e wus e lisbaen antel e mit yeo.**

3. ________ ________ ________ ________ ________
________ ________ ________ ________ ________
________.

**Sam: If I become gay, will you go out with me again?**
**Ex: Thit's net tha wey et wurks.**

4. ________ ________ ________ ________ ________
________.

**Sam: How about if I go out with you AND your girlfriend?**
**Ex: Dan't bi on edaut.**

5. ________ ________ ________ ________.

**Sam: I can't believe I turned you lesbian.**
**Ex: Yeo dedn't tern mi libean. Ef inyune dud, et wos Ellasun.**

6. ________ ________ ________ ________ ________.
________ ________ ________, ________ ________
________.

Answers: 1. There's no point. I'm a lesbian now. 2. I've always been a lesbian. 3. I didn't know I was a lesbian until I met you. 4. That's not the way it works. 5. Don't be an idiot. 6. You didn't turn me lesbian. If anyone did, it was Allison.

# Booty Stall

Sam came over to his ex's house to plead with her to take him back and ended up running into his ex's neighbor, Stacey.

Stacey's freaky . . . in a scary-yet-sexy sort of way. She's always been very friendly to Sam. It got to the point where Sam's ex used to tease him that one day he was going to leave her for Stacey. Now, she wants Sam to come up.

Did you get a haircut since I last saw you?
No.
Something's different . . . and it's workin'.

Sam's perplexed. On the one hand, it's been more than a little while since he's seen any action. On the other hand, what about his ex? She always said this would happen, and now it might. What would she think? How would she feel? He doesn't want to hurt her.

Sam's lost all frame of reference. He's completely confused as to what to do.

Can you help Sam by reading the labels on the bottles and jars and cans that Stacey has with her? That'll give Sam his answer.

YOU
SHE'S
IT'S
FREAK
BUT
FREAKY
TIME
ON
GOT
ABOUT
SURE
YOUR

Answer: Sure she's freaky, but it's about time you got your freak on.

# Diamante Ring

Sam just got the engagement ring back that he gave to his ex.

Sam's initial instinct was to fling the ring into the nearest ocean. But then he remembered how much he paid for it, and quickly arrived at a much calmer and more creative way to deal with his disappointment He decided to use the art of poetry as an outlet to express his feelings, specifically the art of the diamante poem.

A diamante poem is a sixteen-word poem shaped like a diamond. Here are the guidelines:

**Line One:** One single word, preferably a subject/noun that is contrasting to line 7.
**Line Two:** This time use two words. Adjectives that describe line 1 are a good way to go.
**Line Three:** Three words. Notice a pattern? Action verbs that have something to do with the first line are a great way to go.
**Line Four:** You guessed it, four words. Nouns. It's good to make the first two words correlate to line 1 and the second 2 words foreshadow line 7.
**Line Five:** Three words; action verbs again, that have something to do with line 7.
**Line Six:** Two words; adjectives that explain line 7.
**Line Seven:** Just one word again; a noun that is in contrast to the first line.

Sam's already written one poem. Here it is:

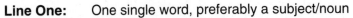

**DIAMOND**
**SHINY PRETTY**
**PRICING SPENDING PROPOSING**
**ACCEPTANCE JOY REJECTION ASS**
**PROTESTING PLEADING PISSING**
**UNPLEASANT LACKLUSTER**
**CRUD**

Now it's your turn! Use the following pages to write about Sam's relationship or your own!

# Garbage Day: Take 3

Once again, it's garbage day!

Holy crap!
What? Like your little ferret friends never come by and get rowdy?

Today, Sam's garbage people only want garbage beginning with "in."

Sam has a whole bunch of ins these days.
Help Sam go through his garbage and circle the eight ins that he should keep.

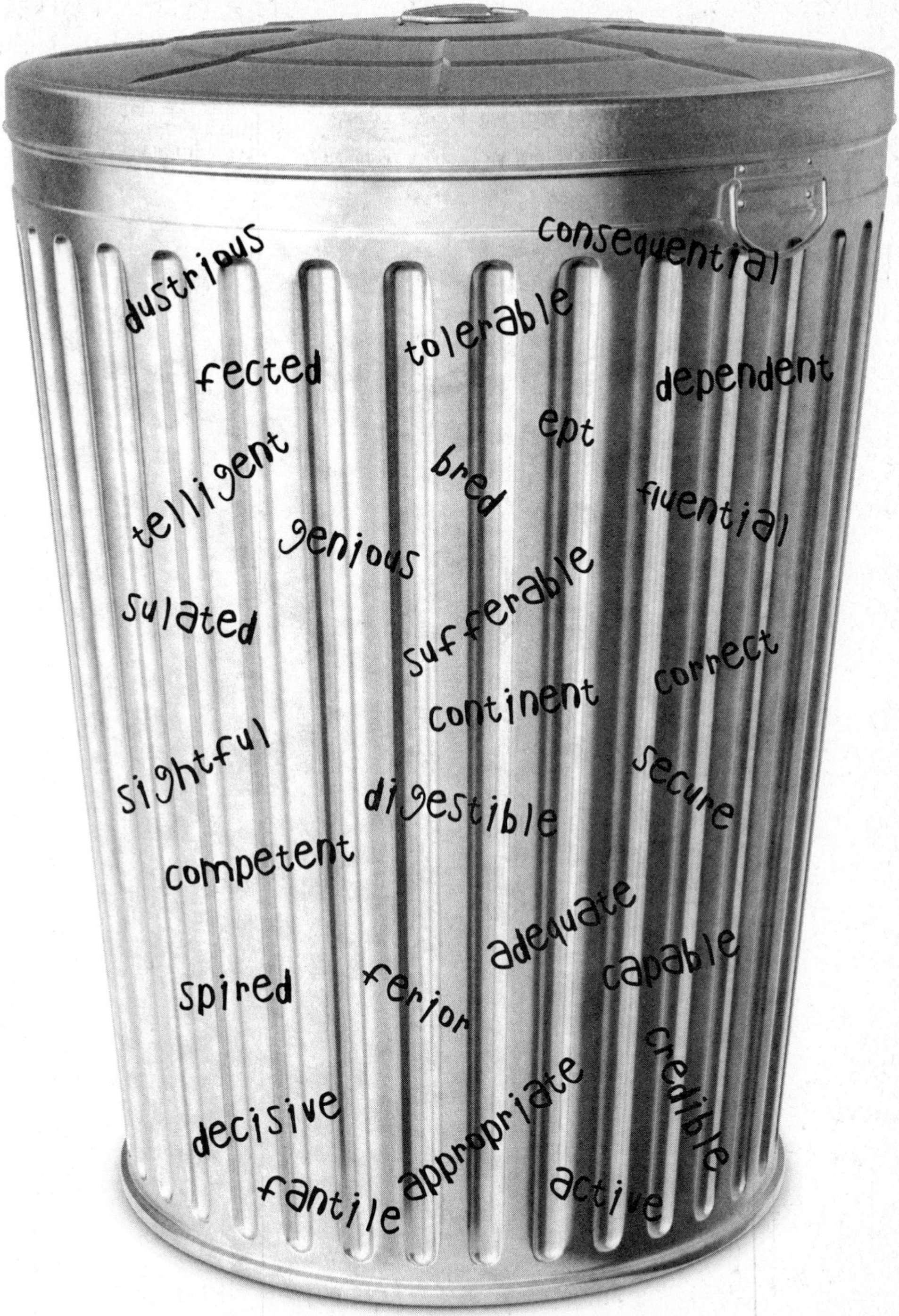
consequential
dustrious
tolerable
fected
dependent
ept
bred
telligent
fluential
genious
sulated
sufferable
correct
continent
sightful
secure
digestible
competent
adequate
capable
spired
ferior
credible
decisive
appropriate
fantile
active

Answers: incredible, independent, industrious, influential, ingenious, insightful, inspired, intelligent

# Time Flies

Sam's trusty clock is one of the only people (or inanimate objects) to observe Sam consistently throughout this ordeal.

Sometimes I feel like you're the only one I can trust, Clock. You're consistent, you're reliable, you're a good listener, and . . . I'm talking to a clock. God, I'm a putz.

Sam's clock is anxious to offer Sam some words of encouragement, but is having trouble doing so because of the fact that it's a clock. Can you help deliver a message to Sam from Sam's clock?

On the facing page, each number on the clock is paired up with a letter. Use the clock to decode the message. Write the letters of the words over the corresponding numbers.

**2 V 2 R Y 10 3 11 5 T 2**

**3 S 4 11 2 10 3 11 5 T 2**

**7 5 R T 9 2 R 1 W 1 Y**

**7 R 4 10 T 9 2**

**10 4 10 2 11 T Y 4 5**

**8 4 T 6 5 10 12 2 6**

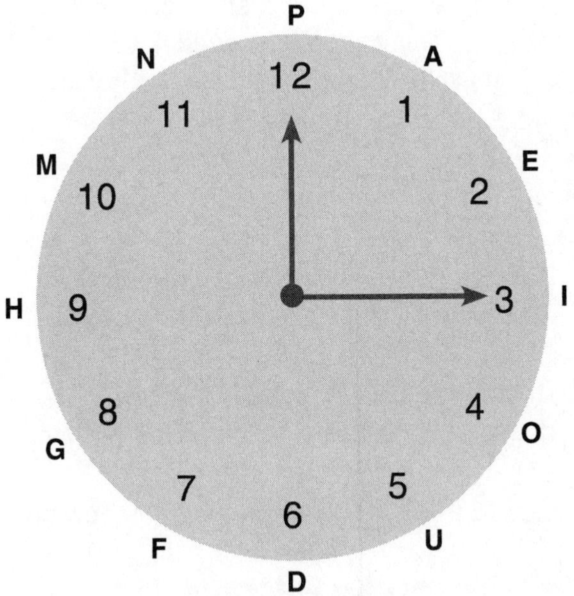
P
A
E
I
O
U
D
F
G
H
M
N
12
1
2
3
4
5
6
7
8
9
10
11

Answer: Every minute is one minute further away from the moment you got dumped.

# Towing the Lines

Over the last few months, Sam's started compiling a list of breakup lines. Here are some of his favorites.

It's not you, it's me.

If you were me, you'd break up with you, too.

Dumper: My needs aren't being met.
Dumpee: What needs?
Dumper: My need to not be with you.

Remember how I told you the night we met that I'd finally met the woman I was going to marry? Well, I'm marrying her.

Dumpee: You said you'd love me forever.
Dumper: Looks like forever turned out to be seven months.

I really believe that this is the best thing for both of us. . . . Who am I kidding? I don't give a shit what happens to you.

Not so much with the being together anymore.

It's not me, it's you.

You should have told me you had a prosthetic leg.

You were perfect for what I needed at the time.

Things might've turned out differently if you were a completely different person.

Blame Jesus.

You won't fit in in Hollywood.

So, just because you nursed me back to health from near death I'm supposed to stay with you forever?

I thought transsexual meant something different.

I already told my family you died.

I'm not really pregnant; I told you that to try and scare you off.

Would you mind if I asked out your sister?

Maybe if you were a little less of an asshole . . .

I told you I was only going to stay with you until something better came along.

It's not you, it's you.

Just 'cuz I've started dating your uncle doesn't mean we can't be friends.

I'm not into big teary goodbyes, so could you just give me back the ring and I'll be on my way?

Dumper: Would you ever marry someone who wasn't the same religion as you?
Dumpee: No. But that's why it's so great that we're the same religion.
Dumper: I'm converting.

# Time for the final round of everyone's favorite gloomy game show—Wheel of Misfortune

I think my body's frozen into this position, Nat.

Vowels! Consonants! Guessing! Hope!

As always, the consonants for each word have been provided for you. All you have to do is figure out which vowels go where.

The clue is: ovation. The message is: optimism.

All right, Canna, let's get down to business. You ready to play?

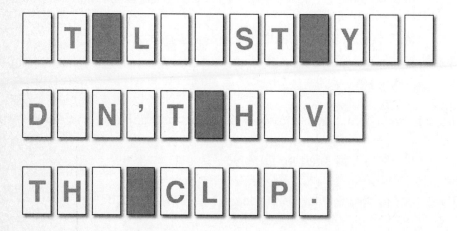

| | | | | | | | | | | | |
|---|---|---|---|---|---|---|---|---|---|---|---|
| | T | | L | | | S | T | | Y | | |
| D | | N | ’ | T | | H | | V | | | |
| T | H | | | C | L | | P | . | | | |

Answer: At least you don't have the clap.

# Dumpedku

Sam's experience with the diamante poetry and lyric writing proved so beneficial to his progress, that Sam's been inspired to further explore his feelings through poetry. Today, Sam is mining his emotions through the seventeenth-century Japanese poetry form of Haiku. Or Dumpedku as Sam likes to call it. Haiku is a **5-7-5** format, totaling 17 syllables. Here are the Dumpedkus Sam's written so far:

**I knew that you'd leave**
**you said you would stay with me**
**you stayed and then left**

**I don't miss the sex**
**missing the sex would have meant**
**we were having sex**

**After you left me**
**I discovered that I'm not**
**really an asshole**

**I want to feel good**
**to feel that life can be good**
**shit fuck piss fuck fuck**

**You said you loved me**
**if you loved me you would not**
**keep all my CDs**

Now that you've read Sam's, go out and write some yourself!

# Dumper's Dialect

Sam's discovered a special dumped secret!

Let me tell you, my fine feathered friend, this world of the rejected is far deeper and more complex than I ever could've imagined.
You've been waiting the whole damn book to call me your "fine feathered friend," haven't you?

Sam has stumbled upon the secret language of the dumped; a special language for the Dumpers and the Dumped filled with hidden meanings and ideas. As a new and novice speaker of the language of the dumped, Sam has yet to master its unique nuances. Help Sam practice by translating the sentences on the next page. Use the dictionary below to assist you.

**Feeling suffocated:** tired of his/her/my ass.

**On a break:** dumping him/her/me slowly.

**Needs some space:** wants to screw other people.

**Totally mutual:** it was his/her idea.

**What the relationship needs:** what my boy/girlfriend wants.

**See other people:** pretend like you/we haven't broken up yet even though we really have.

**Focusing on Me time:** masturbating.

**Boundaries:** how many other people he/she/I'm/you're/we're allowed to screw.

**Strong foundation:** more than just screwing.

**Strengthen the bond:** have a lot of sex.

**Respect that impulse:** have to try not to lose my shit even though it's so fucked.

**Personal exploration:** sex toys.

1. We needed to set some boundaries because she needs some space.

2. What the relationship needs is for us to strengthen the bond.

3. We're on a break. It was totally mutual.

4. She says we need a strong foundation because she's feeling suffocated, and I respect that impulse.

5. I've been focusing on Me time through personal exploration.

Answers: 1. We needed to set how many other people she's allowed to screw because she wants to screw other people. 2. What my boyfriend wants is for us to have a lot of sex. 3. He's dumping me slowly. It was his idea. 4. She says we need more than just screwing because she's tired of my ass, and I have to try not to lose my shit completely even though it's so totally fucked. 5. I've been masturbating with sex toys.

# wedding your pants

Today's the day Sam was supposed to get married. Instead, he's working as a caterer waiter at someone else's wedding.

At least the tux is good for something.

At least Sam doesn't have to witness any of the nauseating joy of the celebration. He made sure of that by volunteering to work in the kitchen for this gig. The only time Sam has to view any of the disgustingly happy occasion is when he's relieving himself. Which he's just done, and is now on his way back to the kitchen.

*Wait! Who's that?*
*Over by the cascading-orchid wedding cake!*
*It can't be! It's not possible! It isn't!*
*It is!*
*Sam's ex is at the wedding!*
*And with her girlfriend!*
*This is serious!*

Sam can't be seen by his ex and her girlfriend at a wedding that he's catering on the very day they were supposed to get married!

Help Sam make his way around the wedding and back to the kitchen without being seen by his ex.

Answer on page 174.

# Open Heart, Tongue Tied

Sam's in the clear!

He successfully made it back to the kitchen without getting discovered by his ex!

*WAIT! WHAT'S THAT?*

Do you have any Band-Aids? My girlfriend wounded herself doing the Chicken Dance.

Sam's ex and her girlfriend are in the kitchen!

The only reasonable thing for Sam to do at this point is to grab a dessert tray, obscure his face, and head back out into the banquet hall.

# Bam!

As if Sam didn't have enough to worry about . . .

Here, let me
help you up.

Love has a habit of hitting us at the most unexpected moments.

The last thing Sam ever expected to happen at his catering gig was to fall for a runaway maid of honor after bashing into her because he was running away from his ex who had just come into the kitchen with her girlfriend.

But that's no reason for Sam not to take advantage of this moment.

There's just one thing standing between Sam and eternal bliss: Grammar.

Sam's so lovestruck that all he can say at this point is, "name . . . my . . . . Sam . . . is."

Sam's so dumbstruck that he's lost the ability to construct sentences correctly. Help Sam get his words in order so he doesn't make an ass of himself and mess up this very real shot at true love.

Reorder the words in Sam's sentences on the lines below so that he doesn't sound like Yoda.

**Samantha**

I'm sorry that I smashed the door into you. I feel just terrible.

**Sam**

1. right really It's all. consider honor I into hands a door the as of someone lovely you getting as at smashed an.

____________________________________________

____________________________________________

**Samantha**

You are so sweet. And I'm glad that when it came time for me to smash a door into someone, it was someone as handsome as you.

**Sam**

2. give Do might think some that number you could me phone your that I you call so you time?

________________________________________

________________________________________

**Samantha**

I would be delighted to give you my phone number.

**Sam**

3. makes That happy me hear so to. You like a person very getting and I look to nice know better forward seem to you.

________________________________________

________________________________________

**Samantha**

Likewise. I never expected to meet someone like you at my sister's wedding, but I sure am glad I did.

**Sam**

4. too Me. you Because restaurant I sushi know like a great sushi Do.

________________________________________

________________________________________

**Samantha**

Are you kidding me? I love sushi a lot.

**Sam**

5. Terrific. for So we go can together out sushi.

______________________________________________

______________________________________________

**Samantha**

I'm so happy that my ex proposed to me, which made me run for safety and smash into that door and meet you.

**Sam**

What?

**Samantha**

It's okay. Never mind.

**Sam**

6. whatever right, All say you.

______________________________________________

______________________________________________

Answer: 1. It's really all right. I consider getting smashed into a door at the hands of someone as lovely as you an honor. 2. Do you think that you could give me your phone number so that I might call you some time? 3. That makes me so happy to hear. You seem like a very nice person and I look forward to getting to know you better. 4. Me too. Do you like sushi? Because I know a great sushi restaurant. 5. Terrific. So we can go out for sushi together. 6. All right, whatever you say.

# The Connection

*Congratulations!* You've helped Sam and Samantha through some incredibly tough times. They can't thank you enough for it.

Thank you!
Thank you!
Thank you!
That wasn't enough THANK YOUS!

Your final task is to color in this picture from Samantha and Sam's big day. After that, you're done. You can go home, kick back, have a drink, take a bath if you want to. But first, if you would do the honors, Sam and Samantha would be eternally grateful.

# Answers to Word Searches and Mazes

## page 19

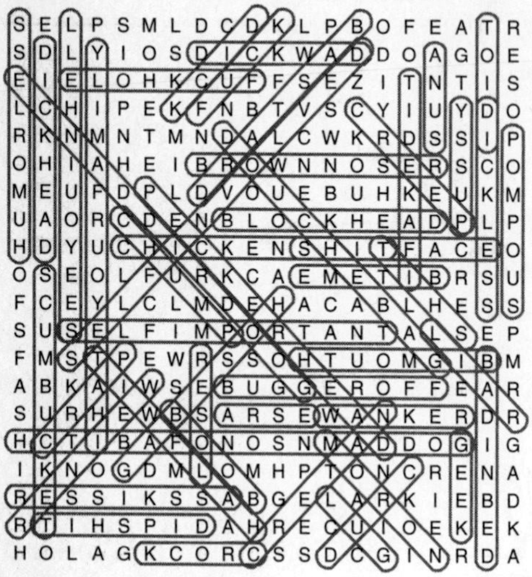

## page 59

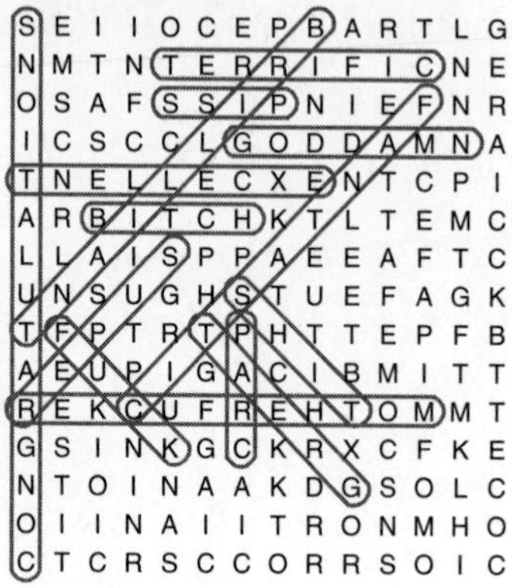

## page 74

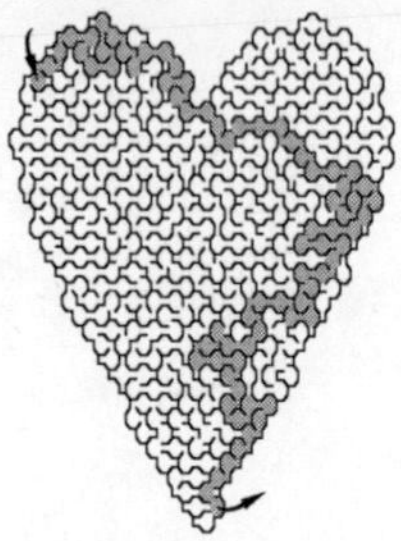

## page 83

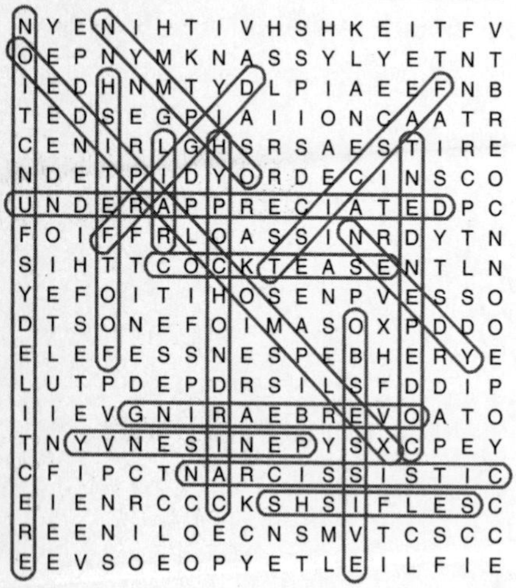

## page 139

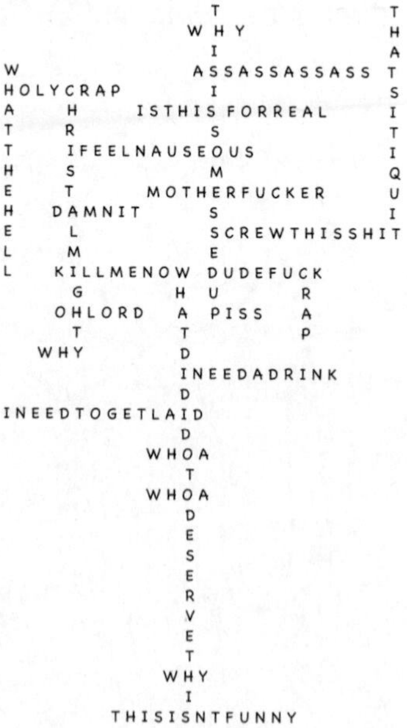

## page 167

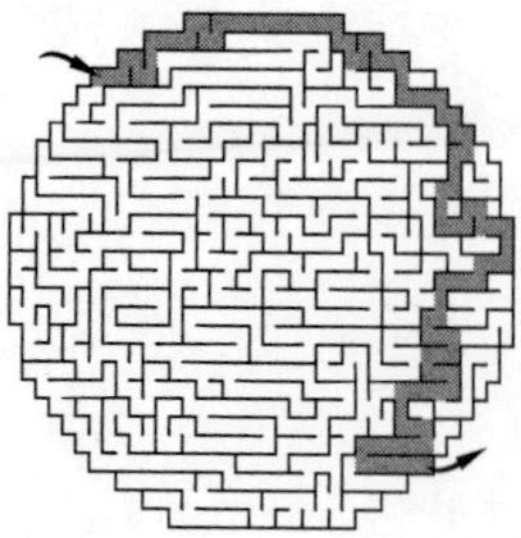